REDEMPTORIST FORCES CHAPLAINS: THE REDEEMER ABROAD

A brief history of those brave Redemptorists who served the poor and most abandoned in the battlefield as chaplains to the armed forces in both world wars. Over 100 years since the close of the First World War. We will remember them.

First Published in the UK in 2019 by Christopher Reynolds through
Amazon Kindle Direct Publishing. www.kdp.amazon.com

ISBN 9781798794579

Edited by Sr. Gemma Simmonds CJ

All images are reproduced by gracious permission of the Redemptorists of the London Province.

Portraits of chaplains are reproduced by gracious permission of Mrs Mary-Maye Lorriman.

Images of the Redemptorist Festival of Remembrance 2018 are reproduced
by gracious permission of the Redemptorists of the London Province and
are credited to Jess Esposito, Charlotte Harmer and Madge Vernon.

PREFACE

Writing about the past and the life stories of real people is not an easy task many people would dare to take upon themselves. This is precisely what our author, Christopher Reynolds, chose to do when he became aware of these men - from both the First and Second World Wars - and their incredible stories of selflessness and utter generosity in serving their brothers in need. As Redemptorist Roman Catholic Priests they spent their lives labouring for others and putting their own personal needs and safety behind those of the serving soldiers. The stories that Christopher tells, from much research and study, are very moving in their descriptive first person tone and from the people who knew them best. Through this work many people will be able to fully appreciate the price these men paid and the fact that they were normal men like any of us. The story this work tells is one of inspiration, courage and determination, all three elements are to be found within the Redemptorist Chaplains of the day, who gave their lives that we might have our today. While many of us in no way celebrate or encourage war, we must however remember our dead and the service they willingly accomplished. I would like to thank Christopher Reynolds for the service he has done to the memory of these War time chaplains. We will remember them and may God grant unto them, eternal peace.

Very Rev Fr Richard Reid CSsR, Rector St. Mary's Clapham, London

FOREWORD

Over the past twenty years as a Catholic chaplain in the Royal Navy, I and many other military chaplains and Naval personnel over many years, have been welcomed and greatly supported by the wonderful spiritual and pastoral care of the Redemptorist Community at St Mary's Clapham, London. Not least, at their most memorable Memorial Festival Evening, last year, to mark the centenary of the Great War. This poignant and prayerful Remembrance commemoration, which reflected on the unique contribution of the Redemptorist chaplains, was principally an initiative of their own, Christopher Reynolds. This book is the fruit of that work. A labour of love, from hours of painstaking research through the chronicles of the Redemptorist archives at Clapham. He has succeeded in pulling many strands together to offer us a fascinating and eloquent living history of those priests of the London Province who served as military chaplains, supporting the most abandoned in the darkest hours of the terrible conflicts of the last century

As we conclude the centenary commemorations of the First World War and prepare for the 75th anniversary of D Day later this year, Chris' work reminds us of the unique presence and role of chaplains in the Armed Forces: their courage, commitment and compassion core to their apostolate. It seems as if such service is a perfect embodiment of the Redemptorist mission itself: to be apostolic religious, selflessly serving wherever sent, that others may have eternal life and know something of God's plentiful redemption. Perhaps that is why, more than 40 priests, from the Redemptorists of the London Province, were sent into the Catholic mission in the Forces. That heroic service of many is not forgotten, indeed lives on and continues to inspire both the Redemptorist community and many more today. As Principal Catholic Chaplain, Royal Navy, I am indebted to Chris' initiative, enthusiasm and patience in bringing his good work, begun at Clapham, to fulfilment in publication and ensuring that the heroic service of so many exemplary Redemptorists is fittingly recorded for posterity.

Monsignor Andrew McFadden QHC
Royal Navy
Principal Catholic Chaplain   6 January 2019
Portsmouth

CONTENTS

CHAPLAINS TO THE FORCES

The roots of military chaplaincy are often traced back to St. Martin of Tours, a Roman soldier, who tore his cloak so that he could share it with a poor beggar. Indeed, the word chaplain comes from the Latin *cappa* meaning 'cloak'[1]. This is to ignore, however, the fact that Christ himself is the pattern for all chaplains. This is illustrated by the story of the Roman soldier who comes to him asking Christ to heal his servant: Jesus offers to come to the servant but the soldier says: "Lord, I am not worthy to have you come under my roof; but only say the word, and my servant shall be healed."(Matt 8:8) In Britain chaplains have been present at battles ever since the establishment of Christianity here. Bishop Germanus was present to pray for the soldiers at the Battle of Hallelujah in 430AD. [2]British chaplains have been unarmed ever since the Synod of Westminster in 1175 but it was not until 1858 that chaplains in the army were given rank[3]. Ranks are held by Air Force chaplains as well but Royal Naval Chaplains do not hold rank in favour of being a 'friend and advisor to all' and in this way they adopt the rank of the person to whom they are speaking. The relevance of military chaplains is sometimes called into question today, however anyone who has served in the armed forces knows that chaplains are there alongside service men and women as they go into the most difficult and dangerous places and situations, risking their lives for others. Military chaplains bring the sacraments to those on active service and at home: they provide succour to families coping in the absence of a mother or father while they are away on operations; they are an attentive ear to those who have no-one else to go to with their problems and they accompany soldiers, sailors and aircrew into the heat and confusion of battle. They go unarmed into danger to assist as stretcher bearers and to ensure those who pay the ultimate price for Queen and country receive the final sacraments and are not alone in the journey home to the Father. Today chaplains are less numerous than in former days meaning that this role is even more difficult and demanding for those who give up their home comforts to go and be a sign of hope to those who need hope so badly. The men in this book all belonged to the London Province of the Congregation of the Most Holy Redeemer, better known as the Redemptorists. They came from all over the British Isles and beyond to follow the way of St Alphonsus who sought to bring the good news of plentiful redemption to the poor and most abandoned.

ACKNOWLEDGEMENTS

I wish to thanks all those who through their enthusiasm have contributed to this book, most notably Very Rev. Fr. Richard Reid C.Ss.R., Rev. Fr. John Clancy C.Ss.R., Very Rev. Fr. Ronnie McAinsh C.Ss.R., Rev. Fr. Bev Ahearn C.Ss.R., Rev. Fr. Dominic O'Toole C.Ss.R., Mr James Haggerty, Mr David Blake and Monsignor Andrew McFadden R.N. I am grateful for the support and help of the archives of the RC Diocese of Brentwood, the Royal Navy Museum Portsmouth, the museum of the Royal Army Chaplains Department Amport and the archives of the Royal Air Force Chaplaincy Branch. I also wish to thank all those who proof read this work and edited it especially Sr. Gemma Simmonds C.J., Rev. Fr. George Webster C.Ss.R., Rev. Fr. Michael McGreavey C.Ss.R., Rev. Fr. Brendan McConvery C.Ss.R., Mr Tom Parish, Mr Darren Lillie and Ms. Natalie O'Hare. I offer my thanks to my family and friends who have supported me in persevering to complete and publish this work especially my parents Wendy and Steve Reynolds, my brothers Robert and Michael and Ms. Nicola Kelly who kept this project alive when it could have been allowed to be forgotten. I would also like to thank all those who supported the Redemptorist Festival of Remembrance in 2018 and especially those who donated items for the silent auction and the members of the Band of Her Majesty's Royal Marines who took part. I am sure I have missed out a huge number of people but be assured I am immensely grateful to all who have aided me in my research and with their advice. This really has been a labour of love and I hope those who read it enjoy it as much as I enjoyed writing it.

ABBREVIATIONS AND DEFINITIONS

C.Ss.R. – Congregation of the Most Holy Redeemer.

O.S.B. - Order of Saint Benedict.

R.A.C.D. – Royal Army Chaplains Department.

C.F. - Chaplain to the Forces.

R.N. - Royal Navy.

R.A.F. – Royal Air Force.

Confrere – Member of a Religious Order.

TocH – Talbot House Soldiers Rest.

M.O.D. – Ministry of Defence.

B.E.F. – British Expeditionary Force.

Novitiate – Period of time in which an aspiring religious brother or sister focuses on whether God is calling them to their particular order or monastery.

Postulant – One who enquires about entering the religious life and lives for a time among the community.

Studendate – A time spent in study for future ministry.

Prefect of Students – Member of the community with responsibility for the formation of students in the order.

Juvenate – A school for boys who feel called to the religious life.

Fr. Provincial – The superior for a given area, for example the London Province currently encompasses England, Wales, Scotland and the region of Zimbabwe.

Fr. General – The superior in charge of the Order worldwide.

Seminary – A place of study for those in training for the priesthood.

INTRODUCTION

In the refectory of the monastery in Clapham Common, the names are displayed of all the members of the province who have gone before. They remain there at the very heart of the community in our thoughts and prayers and yet their words and deeds are often not remembered. One day while perusing the names I noticed that one name was followed by the note: "died at sea." Looking further I noticed two others carried the post nominal C.F., Chaplain to the Forces. The year 2018 marks the beginning of the centenary of the cessation of hostilities at the end of the First World War and I thought it would be appropriate to remember these Redemptorists in a short pamphlet that we could hand out on Remembrance Sunday. As I began to wade through the archive materials in the monastery, reading the chronicles, personal letters and old newspaper articles it became clear that there were far more than three men who had served and that their stories were stories worth telling. Around forty Redemptorists served as chaplains to the armed forces: four in the senior service, the Royal Navy; two in the Royal Air Force and the remaining men with the Royal Army Chaplains Department. Working in the archive room, surrounded by the history of our province, I set about writing a short biography of each man and his service. Some were great military stories, while others were wonderful human stories that touch the heart, but all were inspirational stories of the life of the Congregation of the Most Holy Redeemer at a particularly difficult period in world history. The pamphlet was by now getting very long and it was decided that the book, as it was fast becoming, would focus on seven men, which would include three of our men who were killed in action. Yet, as research continued in the archives, the role of the Provincial superiors became more and more prominent in the lives of the chaplains.

??, B.Benedict,F.Malsch,B.Gabriel,B.Wulstan,B.Michael.
Frs.T.Bradley,N.Cotter,Prime,J.Hull,C.Boyle,Loughman, and T.Nolan.

It was the Provincial who missioned men to serve as chaplains, who held together the province while they were gone, who ensured that they had what they needed and it was the provincial who brought them home again. It was also the sad duty of the provincial to notify the families of deceased confrères and to deal with their possessions. Indeed, they were frequently in discussion with the War Office as they tried to find out what had happened to some of our men. One of the things that really struck me as I read the letters of the Provincial to the families of the three men who had been killed was his empathy with them. This chaplain was their son, brother or uncle and yet he was also a Redemptorist and the Provincial as father of the Congregation here in the London Province felt the loss just as keenly.

These Redemptorist Forces Chaplains were not martyrs, they were not killed for their faith, and yet might we call them confessors? Their lives and their deaths gave witness to the great truth of the faith. Indeed, they were prepared to die in order that no man need be alone at the hour of his death. They gave up their lives to bring the sacraments to the dying in the face of terrible and mortal danger because they knew that the faith they professed is true. It is for this reason I consider these men heroes. If we consider the prophets, they were men who walked in a world of difficulty and suffering and offered another way[4]. The chaplain has the same responsibility, to walk in the field of battle and offer another way: a way of forgiveness, of charity and of peace. They have a solemn duty to bring Christ, the light of the world, to those for whom the light is in danger of going out.

This book is not intended to glorify war, since glory belongs only to the Father, but it is intended to remember selfless service and acts of charity that can still teach us something today. In these pages we remember those who went to walk alongside our service men and women. We remember them with pride and admiration and for that we make no apology. As to those who died so that others might have life eternal, may they rest in peace, we remember the words of our redeemer: "Greater love hath no man than to lay down his life for his friends." (Jn 15:13)

Christopher Reynolds, St. Mary's Clapham, Friday 6th October 2017.

Mr Christopher Luke Reynolds

Chaplains of the Royal Navy, Army and Royal Air Force sing as one.

THE LONDON PROVINCE IN WAR TIME

THE FIRST WORLD WAR

A decade before the outbreak of the First World War in 1904 the First Sea Lord John Fisher had made the prediction that a war in Europe would begin after the summer harvest of 1914[5]. He was no Nostradamus, he drew upon his years of experience in the Navy, observed the tensions building in Europe and understood that the prevailing tactics were to start a war after the harvest to be well supplied and have a short three-month campaign. The 'campaign season' began towards the end of March when the roads became passible again and ended before winter made conflict too difficult[6]. The Campaign Season was an ancient and established system of war: The Battle of Hastings took place shortly after Harold had released a good number of his men to go home and bring in the harvest, which is one of the reasons that the Norman Conquest was a success. According to the established way of war everyone should have been home for Christmas although as we know this was not to be. The Redemptorist Chronicles, which log all major events in the London Province, describe for us the experience of the Redemptorists in the monastery in Clapham during the course of both World Wars. The first mention of the outbreak of the First World War comes on the 6th August, which seems to have been a very busy day indeed for the community in Clapham, when we are told that: "War has been declared by Britain on Germany."[7] The Chronicler notes: "Fr. Provincial returned from Bishop Eton and told us that the Cardinal had asked for volunteers for Army and Navy chaplains."[8] One recalls the words of Sir Edward Grey:

"The lamps are going out all over Europe and we shall not see them lit again in our life time."[9] Fr. Thomas Bradley C.Ss.R. arrived to join the community: he would go on to serve as a chaplain both in the Army and the Navy. He and Fr. Riche C.Ss.R. arrived at London Bridge from Bowness by boat and the Chronicler records: "They were certainly watched by torpedo boats but arrived without mishap."[10] One of the Brothers was away with the Redemptorist students at Beau Plateau, 268 miles away in Belgium, and the brethren were clearly concerned for his safety: "Some anxiety is felt about Br. Esdaile who is at Beau Plateau but under orders to return."[11] There is a palpable and rising sense of tension among the brethren as the news sank in that Britain was at war with Germany: but how did this war begin? I am no historian and will leave it to better men to discuss this event in detail but it may be helpful to have a brief description of the events that led to what would later be known as 'The Great War'.

At that time, the Austro-Hungarian Empire encompassed several Slavonic states, including the Serbians who felt badly treated by the Empire[12]. There existed between the nations of Europe a system of treaties designed to prevent one nation taking up arms against another. Russia declared their support for the Serbians, while Germany announced its support of Austria-Hungary. The Serbian nationalists, supported by Russia, wanted to gain independence from the Empire. The heir to the throne of Austria-Hungary, Archduke Franz Ferdinand, often spoke badly of the Serbians, calling them pigs[13], and yet he was adamant that war with Russia must be avoided. While on a visit to Sarajevo, in Bosnia, on 28th June 1914 the Archduke was assassinated by a Serbian nationalist who also killed the Archduke's wife Sophia[14]. The Austro-Hungarian Empire wanted revenge for the killing of the Archduke and the Germans, under Kaiser Wilhelm II who had been fond of the Archduke, offered their support. This set off a chain of events that would result in the outbreak of war. Germany had hatched the 'Schlieffen Plan', which would ensure the swift conquest of France by invasion through neutral Belgium[15]. Their plan was to annihilate France with such speed that Russia would not have a chance to mobilise fast enough to avoid it. Germany would then control all the ports of the English Channel and be in an excellent position to invade Britain. Britain and France were concerned about German aggression and sided with Russia. In 1907 Britain entered into the 'Triple Entente' with France and Russia pledging to one another support, but it was the invasion of Belgium that brought the British into the First World War[16]. Britain had signed the 'Treaty of London' in 1839 in which Britain promised to protect Belgian neutrality and the prospect of the Germans holding the channel ports was less than comfortable[17]. It could be suggested however that most of the parties involved in this acted in self-defence except Kaiser Wilhelm II of Germany, who wanted to capitalise on the strong German economy and make a show of force to win glory and renown. The German historian Fritz Fischer held that Germany must take responsibility for the conflict because: "documentary evidence showed the country's leadership bent upon launching a European war..."[18] Nobody, however, could have predicted the drawn-out blood bath that would follow. Europe had failed to note the lessons of the American Civil War and the "devastating effects of massed infantry fire"[19], which is often considered the "precursor to the trench stalemate of 1914-1918"[20]. The advent of the railways had meant that millions of men could be kept supplied throughout a conflict: the notion of a Campaign Season was gone. Britain had maintained a small professional army for the protection of the nation's interests at home and overseas in the territories of the British Empire. The British Expeditionary Forces (BEF) came about as a result of the Haldane Reforms, which were enacted by the Secretary of State Lord Haldane between 1906 and 1912. These reforms also resulted in what would eventually become the Territorial Army (TA)[21]. The Royal Flying Corps, the precursor to the Royal Air Force, was in its infancy and had been established two years earlier in 1912.

Meanwhile the senior service, the Royal Navy, had been engaged in a race to build ships for some time and at the beginning of the war was well equipped and so the table was set and the pieces began to move. The BEF was sent to Belgium to help slow or stop the German advance. This they did with an astonishing display of skill and bravery (Recorded in The Gazette, issue 28899, 11 September 1914). At Mons on the 23rd August 1914, the BEF discharged their weapons with such speed and accuracy that the German forces feared there were far more of them than were actually present[22]. The Royal Navy set to work ensuring the safety of British shipping and securing our overseas territories and the Fleet Air Arm, established as the Naval Wing of the Royal Flying Corps in 1912, developed quickly enabling the Royal Navy to defend its convoys from the air, many of the early pilots for this highly experimental division were very young and casualties were sadly high[23]. As the war developed on the front line, the war effort at home also gathered pace.

1914

Fr. Provincial was invited by Cardinal Bourne to provide men to serve as chaplains and according to the Chronicles of Bishop Eton he initially promised twelve and it seems that they were selected in batches. The first fathers to be appointed as chaplains were Fathers Gillett, Evans, Bowes, Stack, McCabe and Aherne.

In the second wave of appointments on the 12th August were Fathers Wright, Bradley, H. Campbell, Keane, McNamara and Cotter. The chronicler noted on 19th September 1914: "Rev. Fr. A. Macabe leaves, dressed in Khaki for Aldershot as a military chaplain."[24]

I am sure to some of the younger men the life of the chaplains must have seemed exciting and glamorous as they set off in their smart uniforms. It is important to remember that, although of course many were keen to volunteer, it was the Provincial who missioned men to serve as chaplains. As apostolic religious it is vital that Redemptorists remain apostles, coming from the Greek, *apostolos*, which means 'sent'!

For the community in Clapham, life continued in much the same way as it had before but this started to change as 1914 progressed. Redemptorists from Belgium were arriving with their students as they fled the fighting. Rev. Br. Esdaile arrived in Bishop Eton on 23rd August having escaped Belgium on foot and having abandoned his possessions. Students were sent on to the community in Perth but were soon ordered back to Belgium to fight and the chronicles do not tell us whether they ever made it through the war. Fr. Evans and Fr. Bowes received appointments to the Scottish Regiments. Fr. Bradley was sent as chaplain to the nearby base at Purfleet. He transferred to the navy very quickly, being a descendent of Captain Hardy of the *Victory*, this seems appropriate.

Mention of the chaplains passing through the community as they went to the front becomes common now and we also meet Belgian, Irish and eventually American chaplains travelling to the front line. Some of the arrivals had been captives of the Germans and it must have been a relief to pass the enclosure door and know that, for now at least, they were safe, the chronicles note one such group of new arrivals: "One was a Belgian soldier who escaped dressed as a German; another was a Redemptorist military chaplain, who had been a prisoner and escaped; another was a lay brother, Br. Anselm, attached to this community."[25]More and more Belgian refugee priests arrived over the following months. At the same time more and more Redemptorist forces chaplains travelled to the front line including Fr. Aherne, Fr. Bowes, Fr. Kavanagh, Fr. Evans, Fr. Wright and Fr. Stack. The first man in the front line was Fr. Jack Evans, who wrote on 9th November to say he had been ordered to embark for France: "Bravo Bishop Eton's volunteer, the first to go to the front!"[26]

FR. Jack Evans
C. . .R.
as Juvenist at
Limerick in
1893.

Fr. Wright initially took his place with the Clyde defences and left for Glasgow on 13th November. On 2nd December the parish held a Solemn Requiem Mass for the repose of the soul of Lance Corporal John McKenzie, who had served as an altar boy at St. Mary's Clapham for 12 years, a sad day for the parish. The difficulties of controlling food supplies meant that the community had to become more self-sufficient and so vegetables were planted in the garden. Obtaining fish to eat on Fridays became very hard and so the Bishop had to take steps:

"Owing to the difficulty in obtaining fish in certain districts on account of the war on sea as well as on land His Lordship the Bishop has dispensed the abstinence on all days except Ash Wednesday and Good Friday until further notice."[27]

This dispensation was gratefully received by the community but there does seem to have been a sense of guilt around indulging in it: "To-day is Friday and we availed ourselves of the dispensation – of course we make up for this in other ways."[28] In a life of scrupulously following the Rule we can understand the way the brothers may have felt over breaching any part of it, even if it was unavoidable.

1915

In March 1915, the men of Bishop Eton received some fascinating letters from the front from Fr. Bowes. The visits from the men at the front were cheering for the communities and in Bishop Eton Fr. McCabe and Fr. Keane visited, giving their first-hand accounts of life at the front.

Bishop Eton before the additional wing was built in 1912 for the Juvenate. This wing now (since 1950) part of Retreat House. Note former greenhouse.

Meanwhile in Clapham the community were experiencing the beginning of the Zeppelin raids. As the Chronicles relate, these attacks began as early as 1915 and the first attack over Great Yarmouth was able to proceed without difficulty. The British anti-aircraft gunners found it difficult to find the zeppelins in the dark. When raids commenced on London the men of

Clapham did not rush down a stair to the cellar to safety, no, they ran to the roof to see the zeppelins and the chronicles record a number of such moments of madness. The fear that would grip London during the Blitz during the Second World War had not yet taken hold. The first mention of zeppelin raids in the Chronicles comes on 1st June 1915: "German zeppelins made a raid in certain outlying districts of London last night, dropping bombs. Particulars were withheld from the public."[29] On 12th June 1915 the community received an important piece of war time equipment: "Most of us are supplied with respirators and a stock of anti-gas preparation to moisten them with is kept in a convenient place."[30] The reason for this delivery is made clear by the chronicler: "The Germans have been using asphyxiating gasses on a very large scale against the British, Belgians, French and Russians. They have threatened to destroy London by a zeppelin raid."[31] The chronicler even makes note of the kinds of weapons the zeppelins were armed with: "They have all sorts of bombs, which they drop from their air ships. Cloud bombs, for concealing themselves in, incendiary bombs, which set houses on fire, explosive bombs, which destroy buildings and asphyxiating bombs for choking innocent non-combatants."[32]

Soon afterwards on 15th July Fr. David Aherne returned from the front on leave, he had served with the British troops at Neuve Chapelle. One of the Juvenists, young men wished to become Redemptorists and who were being educated for their future ministry, Bernard (Buster) Keaton was called up for service in the army and served with the Royal Munster Fusiliers.

Juvenate. Bishop Eton.

The Irish Regiments were disbanded in 1922 following the formation of the Irish Free State and their colours were presented to the King at Windsor where they would remain[33]. Fr. Stack returned in August from the trenches where he had been ministering to the soldiers on the front line. Catholic chaplains won the respect of many through their service on the front line. The need to provide the Sacrament of Extreme Unction to fallen soldiers meant they remained close to their men wherever they went[34]. Catholic chaplains were also instrumental in improving the position of Catholic soldiers who were considered to be: "outside the mainstream of national social and religious life... because of their subjection to the spiritual authority of the Catholic Church."[35] Fr. Macabe C.Ss.R. who had served with the Inniskillings Regiment for eighteen months without rest, was finally relieved and appointed Base Chaplain. Upon arrival his predecessor advised him that the men were not permitted to attend Mass and took the opportunity to remind the Commanding Officer of the promise made to his Irish soldiers that they would be able to attend the Sacraments on active service. Fearing an adverse effect on recruitment the Commanding Officer permitted the soldiers to attend Mass from then on[36]. In the Royal Navy Fr. Bradley C.Ss.R. would be a leading figure in establishing better conditions for Catholic chaplains at sea[37]. On 17th August 1915 the chronicles note that the first British transport ship had been sunk: "The first British transport ship to be sunk was the *Royal Edmund*; she was torpedoed last Saturday in the Aegean Sea, over 1000 soldiers are lost."[38] Two days later the nominations for the new appointments arrived from Fr. General by telegram announcing that Fr. John Charlton was to replace Fr. Joseph Hull as Fr. Provincial bringing in the man who would serve as Provincial during the remainder of the First and during the Second World War. Fr. Charlton took up office in Clapham the very next day, with Fr. Hull returning to Liverpool. At the beginning of September the community were "disturbed by the zeppelins"[39]. A further raid on London claimed the lives of 37 people with around 150 injured. October saw Fr. Kavanagh take up his new posting on the Eastern Front and further zeppelin raids over London: "We were at recreation at the time when the London guns began to make themselves heard. We went up to the roof and saw the search lights busy in the sky."[40] It seems terrifying to think of the community on the roof watching but actually only minor damage was caused: "slight damage done, no public buildings had been hit, 8 people killed (2 women and 6 men) and 34 were injured."[41] There was a second raid later that night killing 55 and injuring a further 100 people. On 4th November 1915 Fr. Evans finally got to come home on leave having been at the front since he left at the start of the war, the chronicles report that he: "looks exceedingly well and strong."[42]

1916

As we enter 1916, Fr. Charles Watson departed for the front for the first time on 21st February. On St. Patrick's day Fr. Gorman preached to the Irish Guards and after the service His Majesty the King distributed shamrocks to the soldiers. In March conscription was brought in and even the Redemptorists received call up papers, although of course once they presented themselves and showed that they were priests they were not required to serve, Fr. Provincial even received his call up papers. This year would witness an enormous loss of life with both the Battle of Jutland upon the waves and the Battle of the Somme on dry land. Indeed, on 31st May the chronicles simply note: "Big naval battle today."[43] This was of course Jutland and Fr. Bradley was able to return on 10th June. The community had feared him lost: it was difficult to keep track of which ship he was serving in because he moved about the squadron quite a lot and he had previously been on board one of the vessels that was lost during the battle. In September Fr. Oliver Vassall-Phillips returned for a well-earned break having served on hospital ships in Greek waters. Fr. Oliver was educated at Eton and then Balliol College, Oxford, and entered the Congregation shortly after being received into the church. Shortly before the outbreak of war he had been sent to Egypt for health reasons, presumably to benefit from the warm, dry weather. He returned in 1914 before being appointed a chaplain in 1915 and spent much of his time on hospital ships, although he also served on the front line in Egypt. Demobilised from the forces on 24th May 1919 he set to work preaching and writing. He was well known for his works: *The*

Mustard Tree, *Catholic Christianity* and *The Mother of God*. However, his main legacy must remain his zeal for souls.

During his life he received more than 2000 people into the church. He became ill and passed away while returning to England from South Africa in 1932, receiving the fortifying Sacraments from His Grace Bishop Sherry. The return of the zeppelins in September 1916 caused great damage in Brixton and several families lost their homes and yet the community maintained their stiff upper lip and a truly British sense of humour, saying: "Zeppelins disturb our slumbers, paying us a visit between 12 and 1 am."[44] One zeppelin was brought

REV. FR. O. R. VASSALL-PHILLIPS, C.SS.R.

down over Essex somewhere and the chronicler notes: "Some of the fathers had a fine view of this spectacle from the roof of the house."[45] It is a lesser known fact that until October 1916 it was a requirement that a soldier in the British Army have a moustache: thankfully for those of us who are - follicley challenged this was repealed[46]. On 7th October 1916 Archbishop Clune C.Ss.R. C.F., the fourth Archbishop of Perth in Western Australia, arrived to visit Australian chaplains to the forces serving on the front line. The community must have been very struck: "He is dressed in Khaki."[47] He was accompanied by another Australian Redemptorist forces chaplain, one Fr. Campbell C.Ss.R. C.F. who had seen service in Egypt.

1917

At the beginning of the New Year Fr. Bradley was able to get home for some leave from his vessel H.M.S. *Repulse*. On 19th January 1917 the monastery was shaken by a large explosion at a factory in the East End, which resulted in a great loss of life. Soon afterwards Fr. Howard C.Ss.R. C.F. returned from hospital: "Where he been for some time owing to an injured knee occasioned by a fall from his horse."[48]

An interesting fact is that the Redemptorist habit is designed so that the wearer can ride a horse, however with regard to the injured Fr. Howard, one wonders what he was doing that led him to fall. Fr. Howard received the Military Cross for his service during the war and was mentioned in dispatches.

The Military Cross had been introduced by Royal Warrant in

December 1914 to reward junior commissioned officers and warrant officers for: "gallant and distinguished services in action."[49] It was in 1917 that German submarine warfare became a real menace for British shipping and held a blockade of any shipping entering or leaving British ports. This had the effect of making food scarce as supplies were lost at sea and so certain recommendations for the consumption of food were made and the community followed them to the letter:

"Breakfast: 4 ounces of bread with butter, jam or other substitute (dripping/treacle) or alternatively porridge.

Dinner: On Sunday, Monday, Tuesday, Thursday and Saturday – 7 ounces of meat with vegetables, soup and sweet portion as usual. On Wednesday and Friday – main fare as on abstinence days.

Supper: 4 ounces of bread – abstinence portion – if meat is used it must be as a seasoning only of main fare."[50]

Fr. Aherne returned from the front on 26th February 1917, now promoted to the rank of Major. On 11th March 1917 came the news that the Holy Father, in order to celebrate the Golden Jubilee of the re-discovery of the Icon of Our Mother of Perpetual Succour, would enter Our Blessed Lady under this special title into the Litany of Our Lady. The parishioners could purchase a copy of the Litany with the newly instituted title of Perpetual Succour for a halfpenny. On 16th March of that same year the London Province received news of the Russian Revolution, they also learned of the British capture of Baghdad. A new zeppelin raid saw three brought down and the chronicler reports that the crew were "burned to ashes"[51]. The Battle of Jutland had ended the war at sea and the full strength of the German fleet would not leave port again. On land the Allied Forces had gained the upper hand and were pushing the Germans back:

"The Germans who have been retreating on the Western Front

for some days past are still in retreat towards Cambrai and St. Quentin."[52]

Despite these victories the rationing situation was getting worse and the self-sufficiency of the monastery gardens needed to be improved: "we must obtain full value from our own soil in the way of vegetables."[53]

Fr. Bowes C.F. left in March to travel to the hospital in Brigh-ton where he was to be stationed. Fr. Watson wrote on the 1st May telling the community at Bishop Eton that his ship had been sunk off the coast of Malta. The following month he was wounded and went to Liverpool to recover. On 10th May 1917 over 9000 German prisoners had been counted after a British push in the West. This push was the beginning of the Battle of Arras, which was still raging on nearly a week later with bitter fighting. The battle ended on 16th March after heavy casual-ties. More fierce fighting broke out on 23rd April, the Feast of St. George, as the Germans met the British troops in the open.

At Mass on 6ᵗʰ May the proclamation of the King on the Reduction of Domestic Bread Consumption was read out and the following day there is the first mention in the chronicles of a German aeroplane, rather than a zeppelin: "A German aeroplane flew over the N.E. districts of London early this morning and dropped bombs. One man was killed and a man and a woman were injured."[54] By May the community was beginning to reap the rewards of self-sufficiency and the garden was yielding a bountiful harvest: "The crops in the garden, under the care of Br. Cuthbert are coming on grandly: peas; broad beans; French beans; potatoes; onions; beetroot; lettuce etc., etc."[55]

Following the proclamation of the King regarding the reduction in the use of bread and wheat that was still being read out in church at Mass, the community also abstained from consumption of sugar. Sugar had now become very scarce and the community also had to reduce their consumption of potatoes. The community was only experiencing the same strains and stresses as the rest of the public and yet the large monastery garden helped them to grow enough produce to keep themselves fed in difficult times. Fr. Paine C.Ss.R. C.F. visited the community before heading back to the front line in France. Although zeppelin raids still crop up periodically the British seem to have taken control of the skies over London now and had become a more common sight: "A British aeroplane flew over our district today, we saw it when we were at recreation in the garden, this is quite a common occurrence now a days."[56] However on 27th May a German air raid claimed 76 lives and injured 176 people, the chronicles note that "17 machines took part"[57]. Fr. Bowes returned home for a short visit before returning to Brighton to resume military service and the community welcomed home Fr. Wright who had come home to recover from a head wound he had received at the front. A further air raid at the beginning of June on the river Medway resulted in the deaths of 12 people with 36 injured, while 10 of the 18 German aeroplanes were brought down. Fr. Bowes had received a transfer and was sent to Liverpool to join a hospital ship, were he would serve as chaplain. In July he returned to Bishop Eton relieved, his Hospital Ship having been chased by a submarine. Thankfully they had been able to outrun it. A raid over London killed another 31 people and injured 67: the chronicler records all losses due to raids with great sadness. This time 15 planes had taken part in the raid, the numbers of aeroplanes was starting to increase steadily. On 23rd June 1917, the Redemptorists in Clapham celebrated the requiem Mass for Major William Redmond M.P., an Irish nationalist of County Wexford. As an immensely popular figure among the Irish troops he felt he could best serve Ireland by fighting the Germans and was one who: "Maintained that to support Britain would demonstrate a maturity of nationhood and that Irishmen who volunteered to fight were upholding Irish traditions of valour and gallantry rather than supporting an oppressive empire."[58] The Requiem Mass was well attended and reported in all the major newspapers at the time and it is largely thanks to these articles that we know all the details of the ceremony. The celebrant was Fr. Upton C.Ss.R. who was assisted by Fr. Lonergan C.Ss.R. as Deacon and Fr. Sproule C.Ss.R. as sub-deacon.

Major Redmond was buried in the grounds of the Convent of St. Antoine at Locre. The catafalque, used when there is no coffin present, was draped in the Union Flag and the Irish Flag with the golden harp emblazoned on a green field displayed at the end of the catafalque. The *Catholic Times* reports that on top of the catafalque were placed the Major's helmet and his sword[59]. The catafalque was then surrounded with military emblems and an honour guard of Irish Guards were present. The distinguished visitors included Major Redmond's widow. The couple had been wed in St. Mary's in 1886 by Fr. Walter Lambert. There was also a number of Irish M.P.s present. The *Sunday Times* noted: "The service began with plainsong and after the Elevation the choir rendered *Pio Jesu Cherubini*."[60] The service was concluded by the sounding of the last post by a detachment of buglers from the Irish Guards, the dead march, *Let Erin remember* and finally *God Save the King* was sung[61]. A Pontifical High Mass was celebrated in the proto-cathedral in Dublin on Marlborough Street. The celebrant was Bishop Donnelly while Archbishop Walsh presided. During the month of July a number of the serving chaplains visited on leave including Fr. Bowes, Fr. Macabe, Fr. Evans and Fr. Howard. Three deacons were ordained to the sacred priesthood in St. Mary's by the Archbishop of Southwark, a welcome cause for celebration, although sadly the chronicle does not name them. In July one of the Juvenists serving at the front wrote to report that both he and John Mann, another Juvenist, had arrived in Egypt from Salonika and had seen service in France before this. Fr. Aherne received the news that he had been awarded the Distinguished Service Order (D.S.O.) and was invited to Buckingham Palace to receive his honour from the King on 29th August 1917: "Today we have recreation day to celebrate the great honour conferred on Fr. Aherne, who receives at the hands of the King at Buckingham Palace today the decoration of the Distinguished Service Order. The King shook hands with him and exchanged a few words."[62] The following day, the *Daily Mirror* published a picture of Fr. Aherne D.S.O. leaving Buckingham Palace in uniform, looking very smart indeed. The D.S.O. had been so frequently awarded for services far from the front line that in January 1917 it was decreed that it would only be awarded for fighting service and thus we can be certain the Fr. Ahearne was awarded this medal for front line service[63]. Meanwhile Fr. Howard had been wounded on the front line and was in hospital recovering. An air raid over Dover resulted in the death of one man and five injured people. British fighters were seen by the community flying over the house high in the sky. A further air raid at the beginning of September on a naval barracks resulted in the following casualties: 1 civilian death, 6 wounded; 100 naval men killed and 87 wounded. Fr. Vassall-Philips arrived home from the front in Egypt on leave but was rudely awakened in the middle of the night as the London anti-aircraft guns commenced firing on a large squadron of German aeroplanes. The raid cost the lives of 11 people with 60 wounded. Fr. Vassall-Phillips returned to his hospital ship in late September. The raids were coming closer to the monastery and on 25th September a bomb struck the nearby cathedral of St. George, the seat of the Archbishop of Southwark: "The casualty list of last night's raid now gives 15 killed and 73 wounded."[64] A raid the following night resulted in a further 20 casualties: "The guns were very loud and continued for a long time."[65] However this renewed effort by the German air force was met with fierce opposition by the coastal defences: "Warning of an air raid was given this evening at about 8 o'clock. People immediately took cover, we afterwards learned that 4 squadrons of German aeroplanes had been prevented from reaching London by the coast defence."[66] Gone were the days of standing on the roof to watch the raids, thanks be to God, but this was a real victory for the anti-aircraft postings along the coast. A further raid was repelled successfully on 29th but the German aeroplanes did manage to penetrate as far as London eventually: "About 9.45pm the boom of our guns told us that an attack on London was being attempted, the firing increased intensely and we could see the shrapnel bursting in the sky over our heads all-around the house it continued until 10.50pm."[67]

This sounds genuinely terrifying and yet the following evening at Mass the congregation barely moved when a raid began and the sound of the guns did not interrupt the faithful in their devotions: "Everyone took it calmly and things went on as if nothing unusual were going on."[68] Once again the frequency of raids increased and almost every night the raids would go on for a couple of hours and they now seemed to be focussed over south London more and more: "Another raid commenced at 8 this evening and lasted until 10. One German machine seemed to be over our immediate surroundings and was heavily fired on by guns on Clapham Common. The head of a 75" shell was found this morning in the neighbourhood of our girls' school – the military authorities allowed us to retain it."[69] In late October news came that Fr. Evans had been wounded at the front and had been sent to hospital. Fr. Van Wesemael had been suffering from cancer and all throughout the month of October was attended day and night by one of the confrères as well as by a member of

the Alexian Brothers from Twyford Abbey. Eventually on 22nd October he passed away and was at peace. His body was taken into the church and the office of the dead was said by the com-

munity and the Solemn Requiem Mass was sung on the 24th October by Fr. De Ruyk C.Ss.R., after which he was laid to rest at Mortlake Cemetery. The intensity of the raids towards the end of 1917 left its mark on the house. During extensive repairs carried out on the brick work and the roof many anti-aircraft bullet shells were found on the roof and embedded in the roof slates of the church. The air raids continued and in one instance the warning was given by police men riding through the streets on bicycles blowing their whistles. The whole house was roused on this occasion and the raid seemed to be directly overhead. At around 2.45am the all clear was given by the scouts who ran

through the streets blowing bugles. On 4th November there was a Solemn Requiem Mass for the fallen of the war. Fr. Cheeseman C.Ss.R. C.F. went to the front to serve as a chaplain, he was the sixth member of the Bishop Eton community to be sent to the front and Fr. Evans, now recovered from his wounds, set off for

the front accompanied by Fr. Paine. On the 5th November Fr. Bowes arrived home for six days' leave. His hospital ship, berthed in Liverpool, had brought wounded men from Egypt via Salonika. While in Alexandria he met Fr. Vassall-Philips and the two confrères dined with a Greek Bishop. Fr. De Ruyk left to take up a chaplaincy posting and Fr. Hannigan, who had been serving as chaplain in Salonika, returned before travelling on to

Ireland. On 22nd November Fr. Evans returned to Bishop Eton. He had served since the beginning of the war and had finally resigned his commission and been appointed Prefect of Students. On 10th December the news of the capture of Jerusalem by Brit-

ish forces arrived. This good news was tarnished by the arrival of a telegram in which the community was informed of the death of Fr. Bernard Kavanagh C.Ss.R. C.F., who had been killed in action during the advance on Jerusalem. The chronicler records his great humility and kind nature and of his death it is said: "One could not help but feel a flow of pride in his generous self-sacrifice for the soldiers whom he loved."[70] The *De Profundis* was said for him after dinner and the vigil was kept in the Oratory by the community. His name appeared in all the papers and a member of the accredited press came to obtain a photograph for the papers the following day. Father Provincial sang a Solemn Requiem Mass for Fr. Kavanagh and the catafalque was draped in the Union Flag. A solemn end to 1917.

1918

The year 1918 was not brought in with the usual celebration and in fact the community, like any family who had lost a beloved brother, was broken: "New year's day comes in this year amid a feeling of soberness and seriousness, if not depression, which does not usually mark this time of year."[71] Fr. Wright had been gassed and had been recovering in the Riviera. He resigned his commission after three years' service as chaplain. On the Feast of the Epiphany there was exposition of the Blessed Sacrament in the church by request of His Lordship the Bishop to "Pray for the success of our arms."[72] The Blessed Sacrament was carried in procession with the canopy carried by four soldiers. Fr. Geraghty of the Irish Province arrived back from the front having completed his years' service and given up his commission. He was accompanied by Fr. Charles Wright C.Ss.R. C.F. who after three years' service on the front line had also given up his commission. Fr. Wright had received a "very cordial letter of thanks from R.F. Rawlinson (Principal Chaplain) for his work at the front."[73] Fr. Potter, of the Irish Province, returned to Clapham from the front and went to Buckingham Palace to receive the Military Cross. Fr. Evans, now Prefect of Students at Perth, visited in order to be with his father who was dying and who passed away a few days later on 16th February 1918.

Fr. Macabe returned to the front in France after 14 days' leave. During his leave he preached an appeal to raise money for a wooden church he had built at the front and raised over £100. At the beginning of March Fr. Cheeseman returned to the front after a few days' leave. In April the "Manpower Bill"[74] was introduced into Parliament, which would raise the upper age limit of conscription from 40 to 50 but would also call for the clergy to serve in non-combatant roles. It was introduced to Parliament on 9th April 1918 but the "Clergy Clause"[75] caused considerable debate and it was decided that changes would need to be made. Fr. Charlton, the Provincial Superior, offered the Holy Sacrifice of the Mass for the intention of the province, namely that this would not result in the priests of the province being forced to go to the front line leaving nobody to continue the work of the province at home. To that end he also visited the cardinal and the bishop to see what was really happening. The bishop felt that anyone called to serve would only be asked to carry out clerical work and most would not be entered into uniformed service but rather would serve as officiating chaplains.

The fear was that if the priests left the province would not be able to continue and so might fold. The debate lasted just over a week and on the 17th April parliament elected to drop the Clergy Clause, which meant that for the community life could continue as before and the work of the province for the poor and most abandoned would not be threatened: "Mass in thanksgiving is to be offered tomorrow. The past 10 days have been a period of grave anxiety for superiors, especially V.R.F. Provincial."[76] Due to the large numbers of refugees from

France and Belgium there were now Masses offered on Sunday with a sermon given in French and Flemish. Fr. Rowan, who had been in Ireland giving a mission, arrived back bringing with him an exciting cargo: "Fr. Rowan arrived, loaded with butter and sausages which his charity prompted him to smuggle through the officials."[77] A welcome treat! At the beginning of June the spread of the Influenza virus was becoming dangerous in the city and Fr. Boyle, the Rector of Clapham, was in bed with the virus. Some of the worst air raids of the war had plagued the capital causing much damage and no doubt this did not help. Fr. Macabe C.Ss.R. C.F. had apparently been wounded and was in hospital at Marylebone. He was to be sent to a convalescent home in Blackpool, while Fr. Stack arrived home from the front for 14 days leave. On 29th June all the Masses were offered for the intention of the Holy Father, that there might be a lasting peace between nations. In July the influenza virus had spread and now Fr. Ryder was confined to his bed, although Fr. Boyle had improved a great deal. On the 10th July Fr. Vassall-Philips returned home from his hospital ship, which had served in the West Indies and the Mediterranean, and had been stopped and searched by an enemy submarine in the Mediterranean Ocean. An American Redemptorist chaplain visited the community on his way from Liverpool, since the USA had declared war on Germany in April 1917. On the 26th July 1918 came some sad news: "At dinner today V.R.F. Boyle read a telegram from Baghdad to say that Father Watson C.Ss.R. C.F. died on the 22nd of this month, fortified by the sacraments R.I.P."[78] In September Fr. Bickle C.Ss.R. C.F. was appointed to be chaplain to the forces and on 21st September he departed for France with Fr. McCabe C.Ss.R. C.F. On 2nd October Fr. Bowes received his discharge from the Army. Then, finally, on 11th November 1918 the chronicler recorded the following: "Today at about 10.30am the news of the signing of the armistice arrived. There was great excitement and rejoicing in the neighbourhood, shown by bonfires, fireworks and hilarious crowds well decorated with flags. There was solemn Benediction with the *Te Deum* at 8pm."[79] The rejoicing continued for a long time. On the 16th the Chronicler notes: "All this week the rejoicing continued. In some cases the crowds were completely out of hand and much damage was done. Special thanksgiving services at Westminster Cathedral were very well attended."[80] The following day the church gave thanks: "Today, by order of His Lordship the Bishop, there was exposition all day with a procession and solemn *Te Deum* at the evening service in thanksgiving for the armistice."[81] Fr. Davidson, who served as chaplain to the forces in Norwich, arrived home for a short visit and Fr. Sproule C.Ss.R. C.F. had a few days' leave before returning to service in Italy. Midnight Mass on Christmas Eve received a record attendance, record numbers received communion and the collection was also very generous, an expression of gratitude for the service of the Province during the war, perhaps. The chaplains slowly began to arrive home and things eventually returned to normal but sadly not for long. In 1914 there had been less than 20 Catholic chaplains to the armed forces but by the end of the war there were 649, 36 of whom were killed in action[82].

Private Oratory, St. Mary's Clapham.

THE SECOND WORLD WAR

Relative peace had reigned since the signing of the armistice. The League of Nations had been formed to ensure that this kind of war could not happen again. However the "clumsy"[83] restitution demanded from Germany after the war had nearly crippled the nation and hyperinflation had wreaked havoc with the German economy. Adolf Hitler, an Austrian who had served as a private soldier during the First World War, had been elected Chancellor of the Reichstag, the German parliament. The Nazis, a name that would become synonymous with death, were now in power. The Spanish Civil War of 1936-1939, directly preceding the Second World War, had resulted in a number of Spanish Redemptorists becoming martyrs for the faith. During this conflict, Germany and Italy sided with the Nationalist leader Franco[84]. Later that year Germany and Italy signed the Axis Treaty[85]. In 1938 Austria, Hitler's home country, was annexed by Germany and the Munich Conference ratified the proposed annexation of the 'Sudetenland', the Czech Republic[86]. In 1939 the Germans annexed the Czech Sudetenland and by September had invaded Poland, leading to France and Britain declaring war on Germany. King George VI, ascending to the throne following the abdication of his brother Edward, addressed the nation with the words: "Once again we are at war."[87]

1939

For the London Province, the beginning of the new year 1939 brought with it the beginning of a new triennium, the three year term of office for the provincial appointments. Fr. James Hughes C.Ss.R. was to serve as Fr. Provincial and took up residence in Clapham. Fr. Austin Macabe C.Ss.R. who served on the front line as a chaplain during the Great War was appointed Rector of St. Mary's[88]. Fr. Macabe had been mentioned in dispatches and received several military decorations, including: the 1914 Star; Victory Medal; Allies Medal; and the Order of Christ, one of the highest honours given by the Portuguese.

Other names to note in the community were Fr. Gerard Costello C.Ss.R. and Fr. Oliver Conroy C.Ss.R. both of whom would shortly be called upon to serve as chaplains to the forces.

On 20th January Fr. Macabe was inducted as Rector in the Oratory and on 26th his induction as Parish Priest was held in the church[89]. One Belgian father passed through Clapham after spending 34 years in St. Kitts in the West Indies, on his way to Belgium for six months' holiday.

On 10th February His Holiness Pope Pius XI passed away on the eve the anniversary of his coronation, which took place in 1922. His successor was to be the Cardinal who had served as his Secretary of State, Pope Pius XII ascended to the Papacy on 12th

March 1939[90]. He had been a diplomat and all his diplomatic skill would be needed during his difficult pontificate. In his first speech he spoke out to promote peace between all nations and the Redemptorists prayed with him: "Our prayers go with him that his ideals for all men be realized. *Vivat in aeternum!*"[91] The community borrowed a wireless to listen to the coronation and knelt in the common room to receive the first blessing of the new Pope. Bishop Murray, a Redemptorist Bishop, visited the community having been to Rome for an audience with the Holy Father. He related that one day, after saying Mass, he asked a priest: "How are things here?"[92] The priest then took him to one side and warned him that asking questions like that was now a dangerous affair. He said that both could so easily find themselves in a concentration camp: "There is a great fear on the continent of what Germany will do next."[93] Preparations for war seem to have been underway already as the world watched Germany's annexation of territories in Europe. Parliament had introduced conscription but only for men between the ages of 20-21. This affected Bro. Steven, who would have to present himself for service: "If only the time for signing on had been fixed for 3 or 4 days later he would have been 22 and so would have been outside the age limit."[94] During the first conflict the Clergy Clause had caused much anxiety and confusion in the community but this time Parliament was very clear:

"News came from the War Office via the Cardinal, as a result of the latter's efforts, that though the clergy could not be exempt, if they entered their occupation when they went to register as "RC Clerical Student" they would be sent to some non-combatant camp (as RAMC). And this "RC Clerical Student" would cover Lay Brothers, Students and Novices."[95]

Brother Steven attended his medical and was passed fit for service and was expected to be called up in the first wave of conscripts to begin the six months of training. For the first time ever there was a garden party held as St. Mary's Clapham. The stalls were all set up in the boys' school at the bottom of the gar-

don: "The weather allowed of the dancing by the Girls' school and boxing by the Boys."[96]

The celebration raised £150 for the 'New School Fund'. On 25th July 1939 the news came that Fr. General had accepted the proposed new foundation at Machynlleth in Montgomeryshire. The Bishop of Menevia was introducing as many religious as he could to the diocese in order to evangelise the Welsh in their own language and so the Redemptorists who went to Wales were encouraged to become proficient in the language. On 30th July a triduum was begun in celebration of the centenary of the canonisation of St. Alphonsus, the Holy Founder of the Redemptorists. On 25th August two young Canadian students arrived.

They had been in Poland studying the language and had just made it out before the frontier closed. The British and French, observing the advance of the German forces, offered Poland their assurance that if Germany invaded they would receive the assistance of the Allied forces. The following entry was made in the chronicles on the same day:

"The one creed of the *Führer* of Germany is one Reich, one German people. No doubt the Versailles Treaty was unfair to the conquered Germans but to rectify this unfairness and achieve his aim, Herr Hitler had adopted the principle that the end justifies the means. He works up a war of nerves in the world until, to secure peace, agreement in his favour is reached. At the Munich Agreement of last September (1938) Hitler assured Chamberlain that he had no more territorial ambitions in Europe. A few months later he broke his word and took over Czechoslovakia by armed might without actual war, just as he had taken over Austria. Now it is Danzig and the Polish Corridor that he demands. He threatens the independence of Poland itself by Massing great troops on the frontier. The Poles are willing to have a conference on an equal basis and settle their problems with Germany by negotiation. Poland, since the taking over of Slovakia by Germany, has a guarantee from Britain and France that they will go to their aid if her independence is attacked by Germany."[97]

Shortly after this entry was made the German army crossed into Poland and on the 3rd September Britain and France declared war on Germany: "At 11am September 3rd, England [France at 5.30pm] is at war with Germany."[98] Within moments of the end of the Prime Minister's speech announcing the second war, the air raid sirens sounded and London rushed for the shelters. However, the all clear was sounded soon afterwards. There was a further sounding of the sirens at 3am and the community of St. Mary's hurried to the cellars, which had been prepared as an air raid shelter, but the all clear was again sounded quickly. Unidentified aircraft had caused the alarm to be raised. The German aircraft began to arrive at the coast, probing further each time and causing the community to occupy the cellars on a number of occasions. Fr. Rector obtained a wireless for the community in order that they might hear the war news and would not miss important announcements made to the nation. In addition to the increase in the size of the Army, Navy and newly formed Royal Air Force, lectures were given for those who could serve as A.R.P. Wardens. One such lecture, given at Clapham Manor Baths, was attended by Fr. Pickering, Fr. Conroy and Fr. Roche at the end of which they ranked as A.R.P. Wardens.

They would not be required to work in the wider city but would ensure the safety of the monastery and the community[99]. Fr. James Maurice Roche was a proud son of County Durham and entered the Congregation in 1924, was finally professed in 1930 and ordained in 1932 at Hawkstone Hall by Bishop Moriarty of Shrewsbury. In 1937, while in the community at St. Mary's Clapham, he became acquainted with the novelist Graham Greene and was consulted by him regarding his book on the Catholic Church. He was commissioned into the Royal Army Chaplains' Department in 1939 and served with the BEF on the Maginot Line. He was reported missing upon the fall of France in 1940 but made his way back to Clapham, finally arriving three weeks after the Dunkirk evacuations. He served

with the 8th Army in North Africa and went with them upon the commencement of the Italian Campaign landing in Sicily in 1943. He was demobilised in 1945 and returned to Clapham. In 1953 he was incardinated into the Diocese of Brentwood and served the diocese faithfully as a Parish Priest until his death in 1989[100]. He has the distinction of being the only Redemptorist, thus far, to have been a member of the Magic Circle, a society made up of professional 'magicians'. The end of the first full day of the war had brought some painful realisations: Br. Henry, one of the older members of the community, had found the regular runs down the cellar too much and was to be sent to Hawkstone in the country. The community would miss him terribly: "After being at St. Mary's for over 26 years he had come to be looked upon as the embodiment of its traditions.

All Clapham will lament his departure!"[101] The other issue immediately affecting the community was of course the need for men to serve as chaplains. A number of men passed on their names as volunteers but Fr. Provincial then selected from these willing men a list of men who would be sent to serve, two of whom were in the community at Clapham, including Fr. Wilfred Murray who would serve with the 7th Batt. Royal Sussex Regiment and was initially based in Brighton.

On 25th September the new community took possession of the house in Machynlleth and work began in earnest. On 2nd October the two newly appointed chaplains of the Clapham community received their commissions and were instructed to report to Hounslow in a week's time. On the 6th October a visitor came to dinner: "Startled at dinner today by the apparition of Fr. Dwyer in uniform! The first of our fathers to report, he is on his way to Aldershot."[102] Having arrived in Aldershot he informed the community that they would be sent to France in a week or so. A great concession had been won from parliament ensuring that religious priests, brothers, students and novices would be exempt from military service.

This was the result of the diligent work of the Redemptorist Provincial, the Abbot of Downside Abbey, a Benedictine House,

and the cardinal along with other religious superiors. On 1st November the chronicler notes, for the first time, the problem of ensuring the 'black out'. As the air raids increased in frequency it became necessary for the A.R.P. Wardens to ensure that the neighbourhood maintained a strict black out in order that there might be no sign to enemy aircraft: "More than once so far men of the A.R.P. have called at our door to point out where we have failed!"[103] The greatest difficulty was of course the church with its high windows. However, once suitable black out shades were purchased the problem lessened. The matter of evacuating the children to the safety of the countryside began in November and the Redemptorists were immediately aware of the risk of the loss of their education after moving away. The children of St. Mary's were evacuated to East Grinstead and Fr. Costello C.Ss.R. accompanied them to ensure they received the Sacraments and that their education might be kept up. It must have been a welcome reminder of home for the children after they had been forced to leave their families. He was billeted about two miles away from the children and so rode his bicycle to visit them. He had begun work converting a hall into a small chapel so that they might say Mass and had erected "quite a beautiful altar"[104]. Fr. Simpson accompanied the children of La Retraite Convent School to Portsmouth after their evacuation. Fr. Roche called in on a regular basis around this time as he was billeted nearby with the 2nd Battalion the Irish Rifles. Fr. Rice, who was stationed at Salisbury had been busy and had recently baptised two babies on camp. The chronicles note: "Fr. Rice had been studying economics at Oxford prior to enlisting. Quite a different life this!"[105] Fr. Wilfred Murray visited from Brighton, where he was stationed with the Royal Sussex Regiment. At the beginning of December Fr. M. Charlton of the Black Watch came to Clapham. Any men who were sent as chaplains from Perth were enlisted in the Scottish Regiments: Fr. Murray was stationed with Fr. McPherson of the Gordon Highlanders. Fr. Brazier, who was based with 5th Divisional Headquarters in Catterick Garrison, North Yorkshire, was transferred to Aldershot and from there to "somewhere in France"[106]. However on route he managed to get a few days leave to make a retreat before heading to the front, "Religious duties R.C. Chaplain"[107], and the chronicler notes: "So it seems that we have a Captain in uniform reading to us in the Refectory."[108] The year closed with the visitation of the community, led by Fr. Leo Kirk who was the Provincial Consultor, and all the chaplains attached to the community were able to return home to be present. As in the first conflict the celebration of Midnight Mass was forbidden due to lighting constraints.

1940

The beginning of a very bleak year indeed for the Allies began with the sending forth of the chaplains of the London Province. In February, Fr. Murray visited before returning across the channel to France and Fr. Dwyer returned home apparently delighted to have the opportunity for a hot bath! Later in the war Fr. Dwyer would be caught in an explosion while at the front of the landings in Sicily and would spend several months in hospital with most of his body in bandages. This did not prevent him from, once passed fit, returning to the front during the advance through Italy. Fr. Roche visited Clapham to announce that, in all probability, he was to depart with the 12th Division Irish Rifles to Finland. However the following day, 13th March, came the news of peace between Russia and Finland and the departure of the Division was called off: "Disconcerting news in the papers today of peace between Finland and Soviets, Fr. Roche will not be going (to a not unlikely death)."[109] Soon afterward he was transferred to the 6th Battalion 'Buffs', The Royal East Kent Regiment in Canterbury, the chronicler noted: "A less congenial appointment."[110] On 19th March Fr. Brazier departed for the front once more. In April an architect visited the community to see about the construction of an air raid shelter for those boys who remained in the school and had not been evacuated, he also declared the cellar shelter worthy. In May Fr. Drew C.Ss.R. C.F. travelled to Clapham on his way to the front in France. On 10th May Germany invaded Belgium, Luxemburg and Holland, all of whom asked for the help of the Allies which was given at once. On 11th Fr. Costello was sent to Perth and from there to join the Royal Navy as a chaplain, though he would later transfer to the Royal Marines.

On 18th May the chronicles note that Brussels was feared lost and on 24th the communities new gas masks arrived, the chronicler calling them their "new gadget"[111]. Fr. Teasdale arrived home from the front, having been evacuated by ambulance, and Br. Alphonsus returned from Rome with bad news. It seemed that Italy might well join Germany. In fact, they declared war on Britain and France one month later in June. On 26th May His Majesty the King with His Eminence the Cardinal commanded a day of national prayer. The community prayed for the King and for the war effort. The next entry in the chronicle is scored out in red pencil. The chronicler had launched an angry tirade at King Leopold of Belgium following his surrender, calling him a coward. Underneath the scored out entry is written: "This item is regrettable."[112] It is understandable that, with Italy entering the war and the German forces coming ever closer to home the loss of Belgium would be a heavy blow to the anxious people in Britain. At the end of May Fr. Ben Brazier returned. Ever popular, he had served with the British Expeditionary Force on its retreat to Dunkirk: "He was in the thick of it but escaped and was full of praise for our R.A.F. and the courage that we shall win through."[113] The confreres at Clapham tell of one Redemptorist chaplain, who escaping the beach at Dunkirk, was forced to leave some of his kit. He had the choice between keeping his cigarettes or his sermons, so he cast his sermons into the sea and made for the nearest boat. Fr. Teasdale who was rescued from Dunkirk and had suffered much: "Fr. Teasdale called, he is still very shattered in his nerves after Dunkirk (300,000 soldiers escaped)."[114] On the 10th June Italy entered the war on the side of the Nazis, causing great consternation in the community. It was described in the chronicle as a great "stab in the back for France"[115]. The community was indignant. However news came that America would assist Britain with materials for the war. They would of course enter the war following the assault on Pearl Harbour by Japan. Fr. Roche returned to Clapham from the camp where he was based in Durham. He gave a vivid account of his escape from France: "Coming through heart-breaking hold-ups of transport, he directed a convoy personally on one occasion escaping narrowly from being ambushed by enemy tanks, enduring days of un-resisted bombing at the place of embarkation. All his kit was left or destroyed."[116] There had been 15 telegrams regrettably informing the community that he was missing in the confusion following the escape from Dunkirk, his appearance was met with great relief. Sadly, on the 16th June, France was forced to surrender to the Germans and the outlook became increasingly dark. Refugees from France and Belgium poured into the country and many came to Clapham. Meanwhile the remaining children of the schools in Clapham were to be evacuated to Cornwall. Fr. Rector went on ahead to be there when they arrived as a friendly face and to ensure everything was done properly, however it had been a fiasco and the children had been billeted all over the place. Fr. Rector did his best to establish order and put in place a chapel and school for the children before returning home. The locals proved friendly and the children were treated well, Fr. Rector hired coaches that would bring them to church so they could be together again at Mass. Fr. Murray finally arrived home from his own ordeal at Dunkirk on the 20th June. His account is laid here in full:

"Fr. Wilfrid Murray came in, an utterly exhausted man. He had landed at Plymouth at 2am the previous morning. He had embarked on the *Lancastria* but the ship was bombed, one struck the bridge and another fell on the fore deck where there were about 400 soldiers below. He was in the saloon at the time and was pitched by the blast to the companionway, up which he scrambled. On deck was chaos. He called to some soldiers who were getting feverishly into one of the boats to give a hand in letting down a rope to the poor fellows in the fore part but he could only extricate about 4 or 5. The ship was sinking fast and after taking off his tunic, collar, tools and tin hat, he waded into the water, now covered with a thick film of crude oil and struck out for a destroyer which was standing by. While swimming he had to go to help a terror stricken soldier and after swimming alongside saw another in an exhausted condition, with no life belt. This man Fr. Murray pushed along in front of him and eventually the three reached a life raft. The survivors, about 3000 out of some 5000 all told, were put on a John Holt boat which after several anxious hours reached Plymouth. He said he still felt dirty and greasy. He was however remarkably cheerful and very thankful to be alive at all."[117]

One can only imagine the relief he must have felt crossing the threshold of his home. He was utterly heroic in his actions and successively put others' lives before his own. All of the chaplains were now accounted for, all except Fr. M. Charlton who was reported missing. Fr. Murray was confined to total rest and recuperation for a few days. Fr. Teasdale and Fr. McPherson came to Clapham in battle dress. Fr. McPherson wore the badge of one who had served in the Maginot Line, with the tragic motto "On ne passe pas", which means "they shall not pass!"[118]

In renewed efforts at self sufficiency Brothers Gerard and Stephen had constructed a hen coop at the bottom of the garden and the first batch of hens arrived at the end of June. The children in Cornwall were finding it very difficult to get to Mass. This, combined with other difficulties, led Fr. Rector to consider bringing them home. In fact, by the end of July Fr. Simpson had brought all the children back to Clapham. Meanwhile a Polish Redemptorist had arrived in Clapham, who was a chaplain to the forces. He had escaped Poland with five or six students but after encountering the Russians they had been shot out of hand together with another  priest. Fr. Bruno had been shot but survived and was sent to two different concentration camps before managing to escape to Hungary and on to Rome, where he became a chaplain. He made it to France and then escaped once more with a group of Polish men and managed to get to England. He hoped to get to

Canada to join the province there. On 10th July the Russians invaded Finland and the defenceless people suffered terribly. On

30th July the fear of invasion was beginning to take hold and Fr. Rector issued the following instructions to the community in Clapham in the event of the evacuation of civilians from London: "The Blessed Sacrament is to be consumed: Holy Oils to be given in charge of various Fathers. Each Father to carry if possible a chalice. The Church and Monastery to be handed over to the military if required.

Everyone to carry a small suitcase and with a sum of money all should endeavour to reach Hawkstone Hall, eventually unless other orders are received."[119] Fr. Gerard Costello C.Ss.R. R.N.

arrived for a short visit that same day. On the 1st August some police detectives arrived and stayed for some time. They were positioned on the roof of the monastery making reconnaissance of the area. For the feast of our holy founder St. Alphonsus the music for the Mass was composed by the church organist Sergeant George Malcolm R.A.F. The departure of Fr. Costello to Scarpa was accompanied by the arrival of Fr. Deary R.N. V.G. August was punctuated with a series of air raids that saw the community retreating to the cellar. Notices were placed on the church doors informing the parishioners that services would stop upon the sounding of the sirens, a difference from the first

War. Fr. Thomas Bradley C.Co.R. R.N., who had served in the first war, and had again offered to serve as a chaplain, arrived to visit the community in Clapham. In the Parish Hall on St. Alphonsus Road there were First Aid lectures and practice led by Dr. and Mrs Wainwright, some of the community attending, including Fr. Simpson. Later, Fr. Bradley and Fr. Roche headed back to join their units and life continued for the Clapham community. Much time was spent in the cellar during long raids. However, as time moved on things became more civilised as deck chairs were introduced. Tea was served down in the cellars now and while some prayed the office or the rosary others enjoyed playing games together. Spirits were high despite the moderate discomfort. On one occasion a sick call came during an air raid and so one of the Fathers donned his gas mask and tin hat and set off into the darkness to visit the ailing parishioner.

1941

Due to the hardships endured during the first year of the Blitz it was deemed impossible to keep the Chronicles and so there is a large gap. The chronicles resume on 22nd October 1941 and "a confrère new to this community now takes over the duties of chronicler."[120] On 23rd October Fr. Oliver Conroy left Clapham to begin his service as a chaplain to the Royal Air Force. He travelled by rail and then by air to the Air Station on the Shetland Islands where he was to be stationed. He had been the Curate of the parish for some time and he would be sorely missed by the parish. The chronicler notes: "We wish him success in his new undertaking, and trust that life in the Shetlands will not be too lonely and dreary after five years in the heart of London."[121] One wonders if it might in fact have been a welcome break from constant air raids and crowded shelters. One Fr. Francis, who had been a guest at Clapham for the preceding month, also left to join the R.A.F. as a chaplain. On 28th October the community held special prayers for the cause for the canonisation of Venerable Peter Donders, the Apostle to the Lepers. Peter Donders was a Redemptorist from Holland who went to minister to Lepers and remained with them until he died and since that time Venerable Peter has been raised to Blessed Peter Donders. Fr. Rice C.Ss.R. C.F. came to visit the community from Dorking for the night before returning to his barracks. On 2nd November there was a raid, the first for three months, and hopes were high that the Blitz was coming to an end. Fr. Roche came to visit as his unit was stationed close by and he was to become a regular visitor at this time. On 7th November the community had to go without meat or fish for supper, the chronicler notes: "We certainly realized today, that there was a war on."[122] However the Redemptoristine nuns in Chudleigh came to the rescue and provided twenty fresh eggs, each confrère receiving two fresh eggs for supper, a veritable treat!

This piece of good fortune was followed by two pieces of bad news: Fr. Aherne, who had served with distinction in the first conflict and was now in community at Perth, had received the Last Sacraments; secondly the community in Sunderland at St. Benet's had suffered a disaster as the school and parish hall had been badly damaged and the monastery and church roofs had both suffered damage during an air raid. The community in Clapham was heartened by a visit from Fr. Dwyer C.Ss.R. C.F. who had travelled all the way from Orkney to be with them, a journey of over 29 hours That same day Fr. Provincial travelled to Highgate to celebrate the centenary of the foundation of the English Province of the Passionists. On 10th November it was announced that Fr. David Aherne D.S.O. had passed away. He was described as one of the pillars of the province: "As long as his health permitted he was ready to give every ounce of his energy to saving souls."[123] He suffered from cancer of the throat at the end and after a long illness borne with "heroic patience"[124] the province felt: "Fr. Aherne has now received the crown awaiting every true Redemptorist."[125] On the 12th November the jubilee celebrations for Fr. Nicholson were celebrated, which must have been joyous for the community. In his long ministry he had preached: 925

missions; 200 retreats to nuns; 25 clergy retreats and given hundreds of lectures. That record would surely make many a Redemptorist jealous. The news arrived soon afterwards of the sinking of the *Ark Royal* but this was quickly followed up by the news that the American Neutrality Bill had been revised and that US merchant ships could now be armed and could sail into

British and Allied ports. On 16th November a Solemn Requiem Mass was held for all who had died during the war. The end of November brought good news: Fr. Costello R.N. arrived from Scarpa with photographs of the inspection of his ship by His Majesty the King; and in Libya fighting was progressing well and it appeared that victory would come over the German desert forces. At the beginning of December some shocking news came: "We have just heard, by wireless, the very startling news that Japan has bombarded American shipping in the Pacific."[126] This of course was the bombing of Pearl Harbour and it was this event that led the Americans to enter the war on the Allied side. The following day Japan declared war on America and the British Empire: "This brings all the big powers of the world into the present war, and will mean a hard and still more prolonged struggle for each country. The method followed by Japan was that employed by his axis partner Hitler, a surprise attack followed by a formal declaration of war."[127] On the 10th December further bad news came: the Royal Naval vessels HMS *Prince of Wales* and HMS *Repulse* were sunk by Japanese bombs, however most of the sailors were saved. The following day Germany and Italy declared war on America. Fr. Costello R.N. and Fr. Gilbert Smith R.N. came to stay and brought the news that the Russians had pushed back the Germans and inflicted heavy losses. Over Christmas a few chaplains managed to get back to visit their confrères including Fr. Roche, Fr. Edward Gibson and Fr. Murray. The Chronicles close the year with optimism, the situation for the Allies seemed favourable except in the South Pacific and Churchill and Eisenhower had both given rousing speeches extolling courage and hope for the coming year.

1942

Fr. Edward Gibson and Fr. Costello opened the new year with a visit to Clapham, Fr. Costello would for the time being be able to spend every third Friday and Saturday with his confrères. On 19th January the army chaplains of the London area had their monthly retreat in the monastery in Clapham, preached by Fr. Wright who had served as a chaplain during the first conflict. Fr. Brazier, Fr. Costello and Fr. Murray also visited during January on leave from the forces. In February the army chaplains' retreat was once again delivered by Fr. Wright. Fr. Conroy R.A.F. and Fr. Dwyer arrived home from Orkney and the Shetlands to spend their leave in London. Fr. Provincial travelled the short distance to the Notre Dame Convent on the South side of Clapham Common to say Mass for the French Forces billeted there. In March the army chaplains received their retreat from Fr. Prime, who had served as a chaplain to the forces, he would also preach the retreat in April. These retreats had been a success in all but one aspect. The food situation was becoming difficult and the chaplains had eaten the community's joint of meat, that was to last them all week. Other arrangements were to be made to feed the hungry chaplains in future. On the 20th April the community bid farewell to Fr. Rice who was being sent to the Middle East with his division. Fr. Brooks received the news that he was to prepare to travel to South Africa, at very short notice, and departed for the Cape. A Canadian and an American confrère, serving as army chaplains came to visit Clapham, they were from the provinces of Toronto and Baltimore. At the end of July the community received news that Fr. Edward Gibson had been captured and taken as a Prisoner of War.

A number of men were captured and in one instance a Redemptorist chaplain, having escaped with a large group, returned to the prison because not everyone had escaped and those that remained could not be left without a priest, an act of astonishing courage. Fr. Gibson's brother, also a Redemptorist priest, arrived the following night at midnight, looking for Fr. Provincial. He was presumably in turmoil over the news of his brother and not finding the Provincial in the house returned at once to Hawkstone Hall. Fr. Simpson was deployed to India on the 1st August. In fact news came soon afterwards that only four of the men sent as chaplains remained in Britain, the rest had been sent to the front. One Fr. Knox, a Canadian chaplain, came to

say Mass for his soldiers on the 15th August. Fr. Conroy R.A.F. returned to the Shetlands and Fr. Costello R.N. to Portsmouth to resume their service. On Fr. Rector's Feast Day the community gathered for the celebrations and Fr. Loughman, who must have been known for his lengthy speeches managed to be brief: "Father Loughman gave a speech which lasted ten seconds. We sang the Vivat!"[128] The Redemptorist communities in the London Province are known for their warm welcome and sense of humour and it is good to see that there is a long tradition of the community living and laughing together, even in the dark moments of history. Fr. Rector brought the celebrations to an end with a patriotic speech and a "final word of victory"[129]. Brother Albert, the Sacristan, received the sad news that his father was dying and set off immediately for Glasgow to be with him. This did mean however that nobody thought to turn off the lights in the church and the police arrived on the door step to remind the community there was a war on. At the beginning of September the Senior Chaplain to the Canadian Air Force came to stay at Clapham and three Irish Redemptorists came on their way to the front, having joined up as chaplains. The September conference for the chaplains of the London area was delivered by Fr. Rector. Fr. Charlton arrived in Clapham on the 24th September causing some raised eyebrows. On the 27th September the new nominations arrived and Fr. Charlton was indeed named as Provincial Superior. On 9th October news arrived from Fr. General to the effect that he was handing over his powers in regard to each province to their Provincial Superiors for the duration of the war. Fr. Upton gave the monthly chaplains' conference for October and Fr. Francis McDermott C.Ss.R. R.N. arrived from Machynlleth where he had been spending a few days leave. Fr. Brazier and Fr. Costello came for a few days leave and departed together for their stations. In November Fr. Lawrence Doyle took up the duties of Chronicler for the house and on 6th November was able to announce that the attendance to Masses and to the meetings of the various guilds represented at the church, for example the Guild of the Blessed Sacrament, had begun to rise once more. During the heavy raids of 1940 and early 1941 many of the parishioners had left the city but had now begun to return to their homes, as the chronicler notes: "We now live in more peaceful times."[130] More good news from the front line in Egypt: the British had won a decisive victory in the Battle of Egypt. The community was given a free day in celebration of this victory. Fr. Oliver Conroy R.A.F. had been moved from his posting in the Shetlands after 12 months to a new posting in Uxbridge and was able to visit the community more often. Arising on the 11th November, Armistice Day, the whole city was enveloped in a thick fog. The trains and busses had to be cancelled and cars crawled along the road led by men bearing lamps. This smog was incredibly dangerous and the local populace was advised to remain in doors. Fr. Roche, who was coming to visit Clapham and was due at six o' clock, only arrived four hours later. However, in celebration and remembrance of Armistice Day His Majesty the King and the Prime Minister both made speeches on the wireless, praising particularly the British Forces in Africa. The chronicler notes that: "In the war, events are coming upon us so quickly that the news we receive at 6 o' clock is old and stale by nine."[131] The letter of Father General was read to the community on 13th November and announced that there were over 500 Redemptorists serving in various theatres of war[132]. Two days later the British Forces achieved final victory in Egypt and Mr. Churchill asked for all the church bells in the country to be rung between 10 and 12 that morning. They had not sounded since 1940 since the men were called away and the bombing began scattering the people of London. However, not enough men could be found to ring the bells, so after the first Mass they were chimed instead by a Mr. Marshall. After Fr. Rector had informed the congregation at Mass that we could not ring the bells properly, and to the delight of the community, a large number of the old bell ringers returned and the bells sounded for half an hour: "At the word of command from an experienced man of 72 rang out the sound of victory for the benefit of the Clapham district."[133] One American Army Chaplain came to visit and was taken out sightseeing by one of the fathers and returned to the house in time for dinner in awe of the black out. He did not understand the strict regulations imposed as a result of the air raids. He said Mass in the evening the following day, a privilege granted to the Americans to make it easier for more soldiers to attend the Holy Sacrifice of the Mass. Fr. Costello and Fr. Conroy came for a few days' leave from their postings. Together with Fr. Roche they represented all three armed forces. Fr. Costello and Fr. Conroy soon departed, Fr. Costello not expecting to come back before Christmas. Fr. Roche, having completed his embarkation leave, returned to Woolwich. A number of guests came to visit, which caused the community some anxiety because the accommodation had been damaged during the air raids. However, all were housed successfully. At the end of the month of November Fr. W. Doyle travelled to H.M.S. *Collingwood* to preach a mission to the young sailors there and returned greatly impressed by the spiritual state of the men. Fr. Conroy R.A.F. had again been reposted, this time to a base near Hawkstone Hall and passed through on his way there.

At Christmas time the community received two turkeys from the community in Perth and were delighted to have something for the Christmas table. There does, however, seem to have been barely anything else: "Owing to the restriction of food this is a 'Turkey Christmas'."[134] Christmas was kept well in Clapham, the fathers were busy in the confessionals throughout Christmas Eve and after dinner on Christmas Day all the games were brought out and a real celebration began. The Senior Chaplain to Eastern Command called at the end of December to make arrangements for Fr. McGowan of the Irish Province, who was joining the Army as a Chaplain. The chronicler made his final note for 1942: "It has been a hard enough year for our house with the war and rationing, but it ends very peacefully with a very happy community."[135]

1943

On 6th January Fr. McGowan arrived on his way to his first posting as an army chaplain, departing for his camp at Bedford on the 8th January. The Army Chaplains of the London area had their first retreat of the new year, which was given by Fr. Upton. The following day an unexploded bomb was found on Clapham Park Road by some children and the area was evacuated in order that it could be removed to safety. In February the house was disturbed by a number of raids but the confrères were by now well used to this and took shelter in the cellar together. For the most part they did not last long. The Army Chaplains' retreat day was preached by Fr. Kirk in February and in March by Fr. Rector. An anonymous confrère, possibly as an April fool's joke, had left a door open which banged all through the night causing some confrères to rise and seek for an intruder, while others still made for the cellars thinking a raid was under way. During this period several members of the community were away and we must assume the chronicler was among them as there a several different hands used to note the events of the day. Holy Week was made extra special by Sergeant George Malcolm R.A.F., the organist, choirmaster and composer for the church who did such wonderful work. On 12th May the chronicles note that the Axis Forces in Tunisia surrendered, ending the campaign. On the 9th July 1943 the Allies began their landings in Sicily, beginning their Italian Campaign, landing in vast numbers. It was at this time that East Grinstead, where many of the evacuated children of the schools attached to St. Mary's had been sent, was badly hit during a raid. Losses in that town were heavy but thankfully none of the children were seriously hurt, Fr. Gilbert Conroy arrived home having been the guest of Fr. Costello in H.M.S. *Collingwood* for a few days. On the 15th July a Polish Redemptorist Forces Chaplain arrived and attended the funeral of a prominent Polish general at Westminster Cathedral. Fr. Provincial and Fr. Rector accompanied him and saw Mr. Churchill and Mr. Eden who knelt and followed the Mass reverently[136]. The number of guests visiting Clapham at this time greatly increased, placing a tremendous strain on the cook and the linen brother who were working very long hours to keep up. For example, one Fr. Casimir, a Polish Redemptorist chaplain, arrived unannounced to spend a few days before heading back to his HQ in Cambridge. In August Berlin was heavily bombed and the Air Force lost 58 bombers during the raid. On 26th August the chronicles note: "It should be recorded that earlier in the month Fr. Provincial received official intimation from the Admiralty that Fr. Thomas Bradley is missing since June last. He was chaplain in the Navy, our oldest chaplain, and was at sea all during the 1914-18 world war. We still hope he may have been rescued."[137] At this time the community also took on the responsibility for saying a Mass for Italian prisoners of war, who were described as: "...tip-top Catholics...They assist at Mass with obvious devotion and love and they sing their hymns with deepest sincerity and they endeavour to show their gratitude in every possible way."[138] On 1st September His Holiness Pius XII made an earnest appeal for peace to all nations. The entry of the 3rd September remembered the beginning of the Second World War, still ongoing and seeming as if it would never end. It is transcribed here in full: "Today, 4 years ago, Great Britain declared war on Germany for her merciless and long-organized attack on Poland. Four years of war and the end seems a long way off, with the whole world in convulsions. We endured many dark days until the Battle of Britain, three years ago, won so bravely and so handsomely by our Air Force, which brightened our future and gave the Luftwaffe a death dealing blow. Dark days indeed followed and our cities were blitzed and blasted but the people remained calm and confident. Now, today, the King has called for a national day of prayer and this afternoon the Catholic Archbishop of Birmingham was heard speaking over the wireless, a message of hope and courage. The Pope's broadcast for peace, made last Wednesday (1st Sept) has made a deep impression on the world, to judge from its prominence in the secular press."[139]

There followed a Day of Exposition of the Blessed Sacrament for world peace. On the night of the 7th September the night sky was disturbed by hundreds of R.A.F. Bombers "making their starry way"[140] across to the continent. As they passed over London they exhibited the V for Victory and to the community far below it seemed as though the whole sky was moving. On the Feast of the Nativity of Our Lady on 8th September 1943 the BBC made a special broadcast announcing the unconditional surrender of Italy[141]. On that same day Fr. Provincial received a letter from Fr. McNulty C.Ss.R. C.F. who had been serving with the 8th Army in its advance through Italy. He had now reached Rome and was going to visit Fr. General. The Senior Catholic Naval Chaplain came to visit Fr. Provincial, presumably to discuss the missing Fr. Bradley and soon the community learned that he was presumed killed in action, his vessel having been torpedoed.

A Solemn Requiem was sung for him in the church and his brother William Bradley came down from Perth to be at the funeral Mass. The homily was given by Fr. Prime and a tribute given by the Senior Naval Chaplain. Admiral Boyd was present together with Pay Commander Brockman. In October a series of heavy raids hit London: "Enemy planes overhead. They received a warm welcome from our guns."[142] Towards the end of November the community was hit by an outbreak of the influenza virus which sent several fathers to their beds. To make matters worse the boiler exploded leaving the community without

heating during the coldest months of the year. Several young Australian priests were accommodated in Clapham at this time. They had escaped Rome just in time and had been trying to return to Australia, which now started to seem possible. The Bishop of Maitland in Australia was a Redemptorist at the time and Most Rev. Dr. Gleeson wrote to thank the community for looking after his young priests. These priests, after spending so long in Rome, were fluent in Italian and so were set to caring for the Italian prisoners of war. In December the chaplains staying at Clapham, one Canadian, one Belgian and one Irish Redemptorist, received news that they would head to the front soon.

1944

In 1943 the Allies had achieved victory in Italy, leading to the Italian surrender, the Germans had surrendered at Stalingrad and the next move was for the Allies to invade Europe and push the German Forces back. However, first things first, the heating was mended in the house and so finally the brethren could get warm. A large raid, lasting around 8 hours, took place at the beginning of January and of some 90 enemy planes 16 were brought down by the anti-aircraft postings. These raids continued throughout January and February, lasting hours at a time and up to 100 bombers taking part. One bomb landed in King's Avenue and Fr. Rector, who was standing at the side door on Alphonsus Road, was knocked over by the blast. In March Fr. Costello was transferred to the Royal Marine Commandos and passed through on his way to take up his new role: "A very dangerous posting"[143]. Fr. Conroy R.A.F. arrived to spend a couple of days' leave at Clapham after attending lectures on the 'Sword of Spirit' at Osterley. He would return to Prees Heath near Hawkstone Hall, the Redemptorist Seminary based in the Shropshire countryside, where he was stationed. He often took groups of airmen over to Hawkstone for a day's retreat. Fr. Kenny C.Ss.R. C.F. an American chaplain, passed through London to assist in a very sad duty. A young American soldier had taken his own life and Fr. Kenny was required to identify the poor man's body. Perhaps he could not face the thought of going to the front and who could blame him? It was a tragedy for all concerned, although Fr. Kenny considered himself fortunate to have the support of his confrères. One Fr. Malone C.Ss.R. R.A.F., a Canadian chaplain, flew in to London to attend a series of lectures and made use of the community in Clapham.

On 16th March Fr. Costello C.Ss.R. R.M. returned to the house. A Royal Marine Commando Chaplain, he wore his khaki uniform with Commando flash and beret. The famous 'Green Lid' is not handed over to anyone but must be earned. After supper he returned to his "secret headquarters"[144]. There were several heavy raids on Clapham with much gun fire. On 22nd March the raid lasted between 12.45 and 2am causing explosions

and fires all around the monastery: "Fires all round us, blast of some high explosives was somewhat nerve wracking."[145] One boy of the parish, at home on leave from the army, was burned to death in his home and several of the parishioners had been forced to seek lodgings elsewhere. Still, despite the dull ache of fear that no doubt affected the community, being a large conspicuous target they had done well thus far not to be hit directly, and parish and province life continued as always. Bishop Amigo of Southwark, whose poor Cathedral was now merely a shell, having been struck during the Blitz four years previously, came to make his visitation and to confirm the young people. The St. Mary's Youth Centre put in a winning performance to take the prize for the Dramatics competition for South London and Fr. Nolan set off to give a two week mission in Lambeth. Bishop Amigo, who was celebrating his 40th anniversary of being consecrated Bishop, invited Fr. Upton to preach a mission in the cathedral parish, which, owing to the state of the Cathedral, was to be held in the Notre Dame Convent Hall.

A mission was also preached to the American soldiers by Fr. Minister at Wimborne. Once again, by some miracle, Sergeant George Malcolm of the R.A.F. had managed to obtain leave to act as organist and choir master during Holy Week, making the celebrations that bit more special for the parish with the wonderful music. At 9.30pm on 5th June, Rome fell to British troops, the chronicler notes: "Intact, *Deo Gratias!*"[146] On Tuesday 6th June 1944, the following entry was made in the chronicles: "British and American forces invaded the Normandy coast in great strength during the night. General Montgomery (Britain) is in Supreme Command of the Invasion forces. The landings were successful and our wonderful airmen, sailors and soldiers (USA and British) accomplished a most marvellous performance. Polish airmen too were in the forefront."[147] Within days the Allies held an unbroken beachhead of "20 miles in length and 8 miles deep"[148]. Their aim was to control Cherbourg, a large French port, which would allow for further landings. The D-Day landings described above are no doubt reported as they were in the newspapers: no mention of the horrors of those who faced the German guns on the beaches of Normandy is made. A number of Redemptorists were present on the beaches, not least Fr. Costello who went in with his Royal Marines and Fr.

Conroy who went in to Juno Beach with the R A F. Their stories are told later in this book. The next crisis to hit London was the 'Flying Bomb' or V1 Missile, which was the world's first cruise missile. It flew quickly at low altitude and was difficult to stop. Fast fighters such as Spitfires could catch them or knock them off course with their wings. The Royal Air Force managed to bring down a third of the V1 Bombs. The community thought that the V1s were low flying aircraft: "We only learned that the low flying aircraft with the thunderous back-fire were flying bombs, when Mr Morrison (Home Secretary) broadcast on Thursday 15th June."[149] The frequency of flying bomb raids and the damage done to the surrounding area led some of the community to remove their beds to the cellar for safety. One of these "doodle-bugs"[150], as they were known, came down in Clapham Common on 17th June and the blast smashed all the windows in the area around the common. The community dispensed with sermons at Mass during this time of great danger for the local populace: "Our people are wonderfully brave and in spite of sleepless nights and danger by day, the Church had been well attended."[151] The fathers left the safety of the monastery each day to go and help in those areas of the parish hit by bombs. The children had been evacuated to the North with only a few exceptions who still remained behind. They held school in the monastery cellars each day and the Headmaster, who had been bombed out of his own house, was now resident in the monastery cellar and had a day room in the guest wing. The bombing was very heavy in July and the community suspended communal acts as it seemed imprudent to have the whole community gathered in one place. Their faith and hope, however, seems to have been without limit in these times: "Our Lady of Perpetual Succour guards us in a most wondrous manner. We have had a few windows broken and a few slates loosened on the Church roof, but otherwise in the midst of heavy destruction we continue to be protected. *Deo Gratias!*"[152]

Only a small number of the community seems to have been kept at the house during this time, members away preaching missions and retreats were also being kept away from the flying bombs. The bombs now had incendiary devices fitted to them and a great many fires broke out in the area. The advance north in Italy progressed well, the Americans were also moving forward in Normandy. The British forces at Caen had begun a large offensive at the end of July and the Russians were moving on Warsaw, although the future of Poland seemed unclear. In this way the Germans were being pushed back slowly but surely on all fronts. One evening as the fathers and brothers stood on the roof a particularly bad raid got underway, since there was not always warning of these doodle bugs. The community was nearly wiped out by one such missile: "Flying bombs came over in greater numbers than usual and several over the house and church, at a time when some of the brethren were on the roof. One particularly nasty brute came straight at us, its engine ceased as it passed over and we waited for the bang! By God's protection it glided a considerable distance and crashed at Wandsworth Rd. ¼ mile away, shaking us considerably, but doing no harm."[153] On 9th August Fr. McDermott R.N. came home on leave.

He had been 12 months serving in Iceland and was to be appointed to the Naval base at Skegness. A Dutch Redemptorist, Fr. Bleys C.Ss.R., had escaped occupied Holland after many 'adventures' and arrived in October to act as a liaison officer between the British and Dutch governments, one of many displaced governments set up in

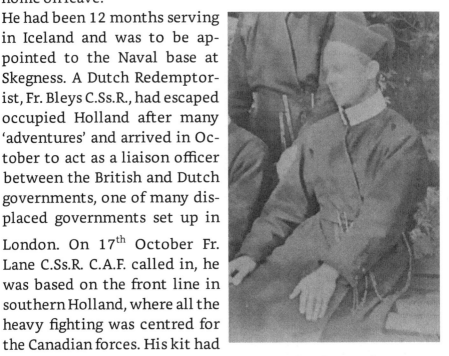

London. On 17th October Fr. Lane C.Ss.R. C.A.F. called in, he was based on the front line in southern Holland, where all the heavy fighting was centred for the Canadian forces. His kit had been bombed and he had been sent to England to gather more. Fr. Costello R.M. made a flying visit on his way to visit commando casualties in hospital. He soon returned to the front line in Belgium with his commando brigade. An American Redemptorist chaplain attached to the Airborne Division called in with some American soldiers and a Fr. Murphy C.Ss.R. C.F. of the Irish province passed through, based with one of the Guards Regiments. On 23rd October the community rested well, their first 'all clear' night in over 12 days. The Senior Canadian Naval Chaplain came to visit the community and hoped to meet with Fr. General soon as he would have to visit the Canadian Naval Forces in Italian ports such as Taranto. On the morning of the 28th October the whole community was roused an hour early by an explosion: "that shook the monastery to its very foundation."[154] The new V2 bombs, the first long range ballistic weapon, were now wreaking havoc in the city as they could not be brought down once they began their descent. At the beginning of November Fr. Bleys returned to Holland as the Senior Chaplain. The Polish Chaplain, Fr. Casimir returned to make a short visit, before returning to Catterick Barracks where he was based. He was passionate about the Polish cause and the Polish soldiers were concerned: "He is very passionate concerning Poland's future and the Poles have the impression that Churchill is letting them down, because of Russian pressure."[155] Sadly Poland would not be free for some time. As the community approached Christmas, the youth group formed a choir and began practising for the Christmas services. Thankfully there was no bombing and the community, for the first time during the war, celebrated Midnight Mass.

1945

As we enter the final months of the Second World War the feeling at home remained stoic. The rockets were less numerous in London now but were targeting areas further north, doing terrible damage. One V2 fell 300 yards away on Clapham Common and smashed over 50 panes of glass in the monastery. The worst of the blast was felt in the Provincial's room, which Fr. Provincial was occupying at the time. He had a terrifying experience but escaped relatively unharmed. The community awoke the following morning to find the ground covered in a thick layer of snow. Fr. Costello returned from the front for four days' leave with much to tell the community about life at the front and of his actions during D-Day. Br. Aloysius and Br. Christopher spent the days following the blast hard at work repairing the windows in the house and making it secure once more. At the beginning of March Fr. Oliver Conroy R.A.F. flew home from Belgium for some well-earned leave, travelling up to Sunderland to visit the community there. On 2nd March Fr. Drew arrived home, his military service as a chaplain now finished, and he was to be attached to the Clapham community. He had served as a soldier in the first war and as a chaplain he had been in France when the Allies were forced to retreat early in the war and fled Dunkirk. Returning with the invasion force he served as Senior Chaplain to the Western Command. On 3rd March a V2 struck the presbytery at Dockhead and killed the Parish Priest, Fr. Reardon and his two curates, Fr. Spillane and Fr. McCarthy. The third curate was seriously injured and the community mourned the loss. The V2 bombings were still coming despite the Allies pushing the Germans back. On 7th March the Germans had taken Cologne and: "all along the Rhine, the Allies are pushing forward."[156] Fr. Duffy C.Ss.R. C.F. after four years' service, mainly in North Africa, returned home for a few days' leave and was greeted by a riotous reception at dinner. He received a standing ovation and blushed terribly. Fr. Conroy R.A.F. was also present and flew back to Belgium to re-join his station. Fr. Duffy returned to his unit on the 15th March and Fr. Costello passed through on his way to Lancashire. Easter Sunday, 1st April, brought good news. The collapse of the German Army was imminent and our own forces were 100 miles East of the Rhine. On the 22nd April came the end of the Black Out and the Russians had reached Berlin. On 28th May Mussolini was executed by Italian partisans and on the 30th May Adolf Hitler committed suicide in the Führerbunker. However, his death was only officially announced on the 3rd June. On 5th May the chronicles record several Allied victories: "Surrender of about a million enemy troops in Italy and the Alps to General Alexander. Capture of Berlin and Hamburg. Surrender of another million in West Germany, Holland and Denmark to General Montgomery. In the Far East, the fall of Rangoon. Thanks be to God!"[157] Finally, on the 8th May 1945 after seven years of bitter war, the notation: "Surrender of Germany. Victory Day!"[158] The community was given two recreation days by Fr. Provincial and enjoyed the good weather for the first time in years. Fr. Charlton and Fr. Gibson, who had been held as prisoners of war, both returned home with much to tell of their hardships. The community offered Mass for the Italian prisoners of war for the final time on Sunday 20th May 1945. Fr. Berry returned from service in Germany and gradually the chaplains came home and returned to their communities. The General Election of July 45 resulted in a Labour victory, ousting Winston Churchill who had guided the country through its darkest hour. Perhaps the nation now desired a fresh beginning but whatever the reasons behind this shock result, the chronicler noted: "The British are a queer people."[159] Fr. Ord C.Ss.R. C.F. returned from service in Cairo and spent some days recovering from a fever he had succumbed to on his way home. Fr. Costello R.M. and Fr. Brazier C.F. also returned home swelling the community at Clapham. In the House of Commons the new labour government met for the first time and sang *The Red Flag*, the chronicles notes: "Not one word of gratitude was uttered from the Labour benches to Mr. Churchill."[160] However, on 13th August Prime Minister Atlee announced the unconditional surrender of Japan, giving cause for celebration once more. The service offered by the Redemptorist chaplains was a true embodiment of the charism of the Congregation and through remembrance of these men who selflessly gave that others might have life eternal we might learn something of the bountiful mercy of God.

Some of these stories are great human stories, some great military adventures and sadly some do not have happy endings. However, if we are to learn the lessons of history and are to draw goodness from something so terrible we must look it squarely in the face and be not afraid. I believe these men were signs of hope at times when hope seemed so far away. They brought the light of Christ into the black outs and the trenches and they brought mercy in the face of the merciless. To me they are heroes and we will remember them.

Mr Christopher Luke Reynolds

THE LIVES OF THE FATHERS

THE CHAPLAINS:

Rev. Fr. David Aherne C.Ss.R. C.F.

Rev. Fr. Thomas Bradley C.Ss.R. RN

Rev. Fr. Mark Gerard Costello C.Ss.R. RN

Rev. Fr. Charles Watson C.Ss.R. C.F.

Rev. Fr. Bernard Kavanagh C.Ss.R. C.F.

Rev. Fr. Oliver Conroy C.Ss.R. R.A.F.

Rev. Fr. Edward John Gibson C.Ss.R. C.F.

The Wartime Provincial Superiors

Very Rev. Fr. Joseph Hull C.Ss.R.

Very Rev. Fr. John Charlton C.Ss.R.

Very Rev. Fr. James Hughes C.Ss.R.

REV. FR. DAVID AHERNE C.SS.R. C.F.

Born 1871

Professed 1900

Ordained 1895

Died 1941

Fr. David Aherne was born in Ireland, the son of Daniel and Elizabeth Aherne in 1871. His brother Cornelius Aherne also became a priest and was at one time the Rector of St Joseph's College Mill Hill in London. In 1889 he left Ireland and travelled to Rome where he entered the Irish College to study for the priesthood. Finding the climate in Rome disagreeable and with failing health he returned home to Ireland in 1891. He entered the Irish College in Paris and remained there studying Theology until 1895. He was clearly an intelligent man and won the 2nd place prize for Moral Theology after his final examinations: however he later claimed that he was "equal with several others"[161]. He was ordained to the Sacred Priesthood for the Diocese of Cloyne by the Most Rev. Dr. Brown, Bishop of Cloyne, on June 16th 1895 at the Irish College in Paris. His call to the Religious Life in the Congregation of the Most Holy Redeemer came while on temporary mission work at St Joseph's Preston, in the Archdiocese of Liverpool. On 21st January 1899 he received a letter from the Bishop of Cloyne granting him gracious permission to pursue the "Divine call"[162] which he had received. The Bishop seems to have been disappointed and notes: "We want good priests, the best priests for the secular mission, quite as much and more than do the Religious Orders."[163] This point duly noted, his grace released Fr. Aherne to enter the novitiate in Perth with his "blessing and best wishes."[164] On 15th August Fr. Aherne was clothed with the Redemptorist Habit and one year later in 1900 he made his first vows of Poverty, Chastity, and Obedience and the fourth vow and Oath of Perseverance.

Now 29 years old he proceeded to St Mary's Clapham where we are told he made himself "thoroughly acquainted with the principles of St Alphonsus' famous system of Moral Theology."[165] His studies now complete Fr. Aherne threw himself into the work of giving missions and retreats and is described as a "zealous, hardworking, indefatigable missioner"[166] and very successful too it seems. He was superior at the new foundation of Lower Edmonton when the new church was consecrated by Bishop Fenton, with the opening ceremony conducted by Cardinal Bourne. His "thirst for apostolic work"[167] could not be quenched and he soon returned to the work of giving parish missions.

In 1914, upon the outbreak of the Great War, he volunteered as a chaplain to the forces and was, towards the end of 1914, sent to France. He served as chaplain with various divisions, he was also for a time the chaplain to the Base Hospital, and became the senior RC chaplain at the beginning of 1917. The hardships of life on the front line are never far away in his letters from the front and on 10th November 1915 he writes to the Provincial, Fr. Charlton, saying: "The Life of a chaplain with the army on this field is not; of course, a bed of roses in this winter."[168] The men of his division were scattered in a number of locations and he laments that: "...with no place to hear confessions, the trouble to get at them [the men] is not small."[169] Reading his correspondence one cannot help but be saddened as he expresses his wish that the war will end by "next summer at the latest."[170] Indeed his voice is tinged with regret as he reports: "Even when there is no big attack you see in the papers, that men are always being killed or wounded, holding the trenches."[171]

It is truly incredible to think that men lied about their age in order to join the army. He closes his letter with a prayer that "the time of peace may not be far distant"[172] and hopes for a peace that will bring "justice to those who have unjustly suffered."[173] In a letter dated 20th November 1915 Fr. Aherne continues to describe the hard conditions of life on the front line in the winter. His steadfast hope that the war will end soon must have provided those around him with courage and relief in the seemingly never ending misery of trench warfare:

"I hope to pull through the winter however wet and cold it may be, as I got through the last very well. Let us hope it may be the last."[174]

Pope Francis says that priests should acquire the "smell of the sheep"[175] and in this effort Fr. Aherne certainly succeeded. He was never far from his men and so was never far from danger, being mentioned twice in dispatches. For his bravery, seeming "indifference to danger"[176] and service to the men in his care he was awarded the Distinguished Service Order (D.S.O.), which he received at Buckingham Palace from King George V himself. In 1919 he procured his discharge from the armed forces and returned to the Redemptorist Community in Perth. He could at last resume the work which he held most dear, that of giving missions. In 1927, after various appointments, he was made novice master at Perth. So successful was he in this role of imbuing the spirit of the congregation upon those men who came to follow in the footsteps of St Alphonsus that he was re-appointed for a second term of three years until 1933. His long years of study and of preaching missions prepared Fr. Aherne for the trying years ahead of him in the armed forces. This experience in turn seems to have never broken his spirit or his zeal for souls.

Fr. Aherne is described as a "very genuine and holy priest, well versed in the knowledge of moral theology"[177] and was considered to be of great value to the missions and a wonderful confessor. His service in so many fields no doubt made him accessible to a great number of people and he is noted to have been an "assiduous hunter who sought out lapsed Catholics and brought them back to the practice of their Holy Religion."[178] He was loved by his confrères: a humble and charitable fellow, he gave special care to the sick and it is noted that he was:

"...the first to offer himself after a hard day's work, to take his place at the bedside of a confrère, all through the night when the precarious condition of a patient required such a step."[179]

The eminent Redemptorist Bernard Häring is often quoted as having said that the Redemptorist of the future should be free for God and Fr. Aherne is a perfect example of this. His vocation was clear and he was prepared to spend and be spent for the sanctification of souls. In one instance, while travelling through

the North of England, he came upon a serious accident at a mine and, in spite of the obvious danger and warnings from shell shocked miners, descended the pit to give the last sacraments to the Catholic miner injured and dying below[180]. He was praised by the local press for this singular act of courage and service but as we know of Fr. Aherne by now this courage was part of his character and it is clear that if ever a man received the graces to fulfil his vocation from God, it was this man. The final entry in the archives concerning Fr. Aherne asserts that:

"He was an exemplary Redemptorist who loved the Rule he had voluntarily embraced."[181]

REV. FR. THOMAS BRADLEY C.SS.R. RN

Born	1886
Professed	1905
Ordained	1910
Died	1943

Fr Bradley came from a Catholic family and was born on 29th May 1886 in Brixton, South London, and was baptised on the same day as he was in imminent danger of death. The formal ceremony was held one month later in the church of the mission in Greenwich. His parents had been married the preceding year at the Redemptorist Church of St. Mary's in Clapham. His family on his mother's side were descended from Captain Hardy of HMS *Victory* and so it is little surprise that he would later serve in the Royal Navy Chaplaincy Service. He was the eldest son in a large family and it is clear that from an early age he cared for his siblings and took this role as their guide very seriously. Within the family he was known as Tommy and indeed Fr. Provincial at times refers to him in correspondence as Fr. Tommy; in any case he appears to have been well loved by his family and held in high regard by his con-frères. As a very young boy of three or four, he was sent to stay with some nuns in Shoreham, Surrey, as his younger brother had fallen ill but notes that he was not there long. When he returned home he was placed under the tutorage of a governess but at the age of 8 attended the local Catholic school for two years. When Fr. Bradley was nine he made his first confession and received a conditional baptism: apparently the Catholic doctor who baptised him in hospital as a new born baby "denied all recollection of the matter"[182]. He was sent to the Juvenate and shortly afterwards made his first Holy Communion.

It has often been the case in large Catholic families in the past that one of the younger sons was encouraged to enter the priesthood. However Fr. Bradley writes:

"It has, I believe, always been the desire of my parents that I should become a priest, if God has called me."[183]

It seems strange in today's culture to imagine any parent encouraging their eldest child to offer their lives in service to the Church, because of the very real sacrifices it entails. However Fr. Bradley's parents gave him their full support and later his brother William followed in his footsteps and entered the religious life with the Redemptorists. The original plan was to send him to a small school in London in preparation for him to go the English College at Valladolid. However the priest in charge at the Mission in Greenwich recommended he be sent to the Redemptorist Juvenate and so in October 1899 he was received into the Juvenate at Bishop Eton by the Very Rev. Fr. Vaughn C.Ss.R. who was the Provincial Superior at the time.

During his time in the Juvenate its location was changed several times: first from Bishop Eton to Kingswood near Bristol; the final move was to Norden near Rochdale in Lancashire.

Fr. Bradley must have been quite a character during his time at the Juvenate and as he recalls his first three years one can almost see the wry grin on his face and the glint in his eye:

"I do not think Fr. Director was at all pleased with my conduct. However though he often threatened to send me away, he never did so."[184]

Despite the levity in his description he appears to have been a sensitive boy and writes of the fear of losing his vocation. He was possibly more likely becoming aware of what such a call demands of us and recognising the need to "acquire the habit of speaking to God as to a friend"[185], as our holy founder St. Alphonsus puts it. After seven years spent in the Juvenate he was suddenly sent to the Novitiate where his fears concerning his vocation seemed to leave him. He later described the peace he finally felt:

"Since I have been in the novitiate, I have felt perfectly at ease about my vocation, and I intend with God's graces to do all in my power to make myself a true and holy Redemptorist."[186]

Fr. Bradley was professed on 15th August 1905 at the age of 20 and on 25th September five years late in 1910 the Clapham Observer notes that "his dedication to God was sealed by the crowning seal of the priesthood."[187] Fr. Bradley was a member of the community in Clapham from 1915 and is noted in the Provincial Archives as the community librarian.

At the outbreak of war in 1914 the Catholic Herald noted that there were 233 Anglican chaplains to the Royal Navy's fleet at sea and only one Roman Catholic chaplain. This was seen by some to be down to anti-Catholic sentiment within the service but Cardinal Bourne responded that he was in daily contact with the War Office and with the First Lord of the Admiralty, Winston Churchill, and in his letter said:

"I am happy to testify publicly...every effort has been made to ensure to our Catholic soldiers and sailors the spiritual ministrations of which in these days they stand in such urgent need."[188]

The Redemptorists, recognising the need to support the 'most abandoned' in this dark hour, offered men to serve as Chaplains to the armed forces. Indeed a note dated 19th Dec 1914 states that:

"8 CSsR students arrive from Beau Plateau, they are going to serve in the army."[189]

These 8 students were soon replaced by another 8 students who had fled Belgium. These students were sent initially to studies in Perth but on 28th May 1915 they returned to Clapham: they were required by the Belgian military authorities and departed for the front on 31st May of the same year. A note from 24th November 1914 tells us:

"A Belgian refugee secular priest, Fr Sansimont, is staying with us just now. He has witnessed a lot of German activities and was interviewed for several hours by an official from the Home Office today."[190]

Fr. Bradley joined the Army as a Chaplain and on 4th December 1914 he replaced Rev. Fr. Bernard Kavanagh C.Ss.R. as base chaplain with the 7th Royal West Kent, at Purfleet in Essex as Fr Kavanagh was being sent to the front. Sadly three years later Fr. Kavanagh was killed by a sniper while tending to a wounded man during the advance of the 60th Division on Jerusalem: he was 53 years old. Fr. Bradley saw service in France but later Fr. Provincial wrote to the War Office and requested he be returned to his community. However, presumably having convinced the Provincial of the need for chaplains at sea and at his own request, he was transferred to the Royal Navy, and was officially appointed as a Temporary Chaplain to the navy on 26th February 1915.

On 1st September 1915 Fr. Bradley was moved to the Redemptorist community in Perth but visited the Clapham community on 6th November 1915. His move to Perth may well have been necessitated by the location of the 1st and 2nd Battlecruiser Squadrons, in which he served. His first naval posting was to replace Fr. Adrian Weld-Blundell O.S.B. on board HMS *New Zealand* as the chaplain to the 2nd Battlecruiser Squadron[191]. Fr. Bradley was an important figure in increasing awareness of the unjust way Catholics and Catholic chaplains were treated at sea. In a letter to Mgr. Bidwell he notes that:

"Some men, especially stokers, are unable to attend Mass or the

Sacrament."[192]

Catholic chaplains were not commissioned and were therefore not on the ship's books for pay. This meant that they were not able to buy things from the paymaster's stores. They would also not receive any compensation if wounded and would not receive any honours awarded to officers in the navy[193]. In fact it appears that Catholic chaplains were simply tolerated at this stage. However Admiral Beatty was in favour of commissioning Catholic chaplains and "pointed out that Fr. Patrick Gibbons held a commission in the Royal Australian Navy."[194]

Fr. Bradley worked with Fr. Gibbons in order to share the duties of visiting ships and said:

"I think it is up to chaplains, who are making traditions and precedents, to make our own position as secure and honourable as possible."[195]

He was present at a number of big engagements. The Clapham Observer notes that he was on "the vessel which took His Royal Highness the Prince of Wales to Canada."[196] Fr. Bradley was a popular chaplain among the sailors but his parish was composed of two large squadrons of ships and so he could not possibly hope to be able to minister to all of his parishioners. In July 1915 Fr. Bradley was based on HMS *New Zealand* from where he offered the holy sacrifice of the Mass. William Francis Jones of no. 4 mess on board HMS *Tiger* wrote to the Cardinal on behalf of the Catholic sailors of the squadron explaining that they had not been able to go to Mass for five weeks:

"I hope by the help of our blessed Lady that you will let us have a Chaplain in our squadron. It is sometimes five weeks and we cannot go to Holy Mass on Sunday…"[197]

The only immediate response to this letter was to enquire of the Admiralty if this was the case. However by the end of the war in 1918 there were 31 chaplains serving with the fleet. One chaplain describes a chapel on board a ship:

"Here, with the help of his men, he has 'rigged up' a little permanent chapel. Against the bulkheads are little coloured prints of the Stations of the Cross. In this quiet spot his congregation can in their free time come and say their prayers or read C.T.S. lives of the Saints."[198]

In 1916 the Royal Navy saw the largest loss of life at sea ever in its history: the Battle of Jutland. The chronicles of St Mary's Clapham recorded on 31st May 1916: "Big naval battle today."[199] The battle lasted 12 hours and at the end of the fighting the British fleet had suffered heavy losses. More than 6000 men perished during the battle[200]. The British fleet was composed of 151 ships split into two squadrons commanded by Admiral Jellicoe and Vice Admiral Beatty, while the German fleet was considerably smaller with 99 ships. Of the 151 ships that put out to sea 14 never returned. It was a shock for the navy. The chronicles report that Fr. Bradley was involved in the "recent naval battle between the British and German fleets."[201] There were six Catholic chaplains present at the battle, one of whom perished with HMS *Black Prince*. Another chaplain Fr. Anthony Pollen in an act of tremendous heroism:

"Threw himself into a cordite fire caused by enemy shell-fire without a thought for his own safety to rescue two seamen."[202]

Fr. Bradley was on board HMS *Tiger* during the fighting, which was commanded by Vice-Admiral Sir David Beatty RN. He reported that at around 1554 hours "a series of shells crashed down"[203] on the *Tiger* putting two gun turrets out of action. A young midshipman was trapped and injured in one of these turrets and Fr. Bradley went with the medical team to help the stricken sailor:

"The poor fellow was wounded in several places. I took off his sea boots and found a piece of shell had gone through into his foot. He was also wounded in the arm and side. His left eye was lying on top of a mass of bruised flesh that filled up the cavity of the eye. He was taken to the Padre's cabin where he died during the night."[204]

It has been suggested by many that the Royal Navy considered that this would be a crushing outright victory and the sailors were waiting to see action:

"The Germans have not appeared yet. About that He [the British sailor] feels very sore. He has brothers and friends in the trenches and knows what splendid work they are doing while to all appearances he is idle...He wants to fight. He is spoiling for it."[205]

This was clearly not the case: HMS *Indefatigable* and HMS *Queen Mary* had both been sunk and had received direct hits to the magazine amidships and sunk very quickly. Fr. Bradley recorded what it was like to be on board at this stage in the battle:

"After the *Indefatigable* and the *Queen Mary* had gone there was the fear that we might suffer the same fate and that one of the shells might get at one of our magazines, we would all be entombed in the ship."[206]

The deep magazine on the *Dreadnought* Battlecruiser stored the shells and cordite propellant, which were elevated to the guns via a large turret. A direct hit would create an enormous explosion causing catastrophic damage to the ship's hull and destroying anything in its way. The *Queen Mary*, it is proposed, sank so quickly because, in order to maintain the rapid fire upon German ships, the bulkhead doors were left open. This made the route of least resistance for the explosion of a shell in a gun turret straight down to the deep magazine where upon the explosion could split the ship in two. The confusion of battle at sea is hard to imagine sitting at a desk but for those men who worked in the engine rooms or in the deep magazine it must have been terrifying. Fr. Bradley describes the fear and confusion of those frantic 12 hours:

"We had a very unpleasant list due to the flooded magazines, We did not know the cause and every time the ship turned to port the list increased and we did not know what was happening, there was the dread fear the ship was turning over."[207]

The threat of imminent death was hanging over the men as Fr. Bradley recalls:

"The hatchways leading from the engine rooms on to the gangways and those leading from the mess decks above are all, or almost all, battened down. Only one other way up is left free so that we had the somewhat unpleasant knowledge that if the ship went suddenly we would be drowned like rats in a cage – or perhaps a worse fate awaited in the submerged flats which are watertight."[208]

During the night the fighting continued and sleep would have been difficult for men who were tired, shocked and frightened. Food was perhaps some comfort if you could get it. One young midshipman is even reported as stealing the Admiral's ham Fr. Bradley describes the scene for us:

"The night was not a restful one. Anything like turning in was out of the question. We all felt horribly tired. The men lay down in any dry place they could find and the doctors, after they had finished the operations, lay down in the distributing station."[209]

His search for food was mildly successful however:

"We managed to get hold of some ginger beer and later coerced the messman's assistant to give us bully beef and some biscuits. We also got some soda water and half a bottle of whiskey. But these did not go far amongst a lot of hungry officers. I was very wet and tired and hungry and bully beef, ginger beer and biscuits were very welcome, only one was impeded by the dirt and blood on one's hands from touching anything directly."[210]

As the battle came to a close and the fleets drifted apart the sailors could breathe a sigh of relief. Despite the heavy losses suffered at Jutland the Royal Navy had achieved its aim to enforce the blockade of the North Sea, the only trade route left open to Germany. This blockade contributed in no small way to the winning of the war by preventing supplies reaching Germany. The German fleet never attempted an all-out battle with the Royal Navy again during the war. In the aftermath of the battle it was left to Fr. Bradley to see to the dead who remained where they had fallen:

"The sight was terrible. There was a considerable amount of water. There in all of this, mixed up with the rubbish and debris were bodies or bits of bodies. One had no head as far as I could see, nor legs, the left arm was gone and the right lay near with its hand hanging off, It was a mere trunk - quite naked - for the blast tore the clothes off. You could feel the little pieces of limbs under your feet as you walked ankle deep in water. It was quite dark save for the torch we had. Later on I got together a stretcher party to try and get the pieces away, but when they saw what they had to tackle they slunk away, and I must confess I was not sorry."[211]

The genuine horror of what Fr. Bradley had to do that day can never have left him, but I think this experience, of seeing how necessary it was to have the light of Christ brought into the darkest and most fearful of places, is what prompted him to offer himself, in 1939, to serve again in the Second World War.

A letter from the Superior General of the Congregation in Rome to Fr. Provincial following the battle of Jutland reads:

"We are very glad to get the news from Fr. Bradley, as we had been very anxious to hear about him. We thought he was on the *New Zealand* which was in the battle, and very anxiously scrutinized the lists of casualties. However it is now a comfort to hear he has escaped, and it is not likely he will have a similar ordeal. The papers here are of the same opinion as the naval authorities there regarding the result of the battle, both from the fact that the German losses seem greater absolutely and are certainly much greater relatively, but chiefly because, on the Germans' own principle of not counting the cost provided they attain their object, what was left of the German fleet was locked up again in the Kiel Canal. Still the Germans still speak of it as a victory for them."[212]

The chronicles betray a slow and steady feeling that things were improving throughout 1917 and mentions of air raids become more few and far between. On 3rd April 1918 Fr. Bradley spent four days leave in Clapham before returning to his station. On 11th November 1918 the chronicler made the following entry:

"Today at about 10.30 am the news of the signing of the armistice arrived. There was great excitement and rejoicing in the neighbourhood, shown by bonfires, fireworks and hilarious crowds well decorated with flags. There was solemn Benediction with the *Te Deum* at 8pm."[213]

Through the next few weeks there processions and thanksgiving services as the joy and relief washed away the tension and fear that had held the nation in its grip. On 29th July 1919 the Provincial received a letter from the cardinal's office at Westminster asking if he could spare Fr. Bradley for a little longer:

"I am desire by the Cardinal to ask you whether you could possibly spare Fr. Bradley, who is doing such good work in the Navy, until the end of this year. His Eminence understands that you are anxious to have him back by the end of September and wishes me to point out that the Navy just now is under reconstitution and until this new formation of fleets is definitely settles (which is not likely to be until the end of December) he demurs very much to make any changes in such an important squadron as the Battlecruiser Squadron in case the Admiralty would not agree to a new appointment, should a vacancy occur."[214]

The relief felt at home of the end of hostilities was great but the peacetime work of the Navy now began and re-organisation was the first step. For 20 years after the end of the First World War Fr. Bradley worked zealously in the Province giving missions and ministering to the poor and most abandoned. He was loved and admired in the parish in Clapham but never lost his love of the sea.

In 1939 the world was flung into a second conflict. King George VI announced during a radio broadcast that once again we were at war. He told the nation that:

"...we are called by our allies to meet a challenge of a principle which, if it were to prevail, would be fateful to any civilised order in the world. It is a principle which permits the state, in the selfish pursuit of power, to disregard its treaties and its solemn pledges, which sanctions the use of force against the security and independence of other states. Such a principle, stripped of all disguise, is the primitive doctrine that might is right."[215]

On 28th May 1939 on his way back from Rome Bishop Murray, a Redemptorist, visited the community at Clapham. He often said Mass in Cologne and he asked a priest over breakfast how things were in Germany. The priest responded by motioning him aside and saying:

"He told him such a question should not have been put to him in public; both could so easily find themselves in a Concentration

Camp. [216]

The priest related that things were so bad in Germany and that religion was being oppressed heavily. He continued: "There is great fear on the continent of what Germany will do next."[217] On 3rd September 1939 the chronicles record that "England… is at war with Germany."[218] This message is underlined in red. What follows is a series of air raids that mainly seem to have turned out to be false alarms. The community of St Mary's took refuge in the cellars. Fr. Bradley, despite being over the age limit, returned to service in the Royal Navy. He visited Clapham on 21st August 1940 from the naval base at Falmouth. In 1943 Fr. Bradley was stationed at Kilindini, near Mombasa in Kenya, His letters to Fr. Provincial mainly concern his expenses, I suppose security prevented him from giving too much detail in a letter which may go missing. He served on a number of ships during this time and notes in his letter of November 1942:

"I have moved to another ship or rather was moved suddenly. This has happened three times this year…going off to another part of the world and then back to London and out here again."[219]

He goes on to request a copy of the ORDO for 1943, it is easy to forget how difficult it must have been for chaplains on the move to get hold of books and materials needed to celebrate the holy sacrifice of the Mass. His life at sea must have been a difficult one, being constantly in the picket boat moving between ships in choppy seas to visit the Catholic sailors: "Ship life in this climate can be trying."[220] However he announces with great relief that he has finally been able to go on leave:

"I managed to get five days' leave (long overdue time) and stayed with a priest for four days' rest – which I needed."[221]

In his letter of December 1942 Fr. Bradley again laments the climate:

"The tropics are trying at first – till one gets acclimatised. Except for a bout of rheumatism due to being out all night in a boat I keep well."[222]

He closes the letter in the most fraternal way, wishing Fr. Provincial a happy Christmas and a prosperous new year. In his following letter he describes what sounds like a truly splendid celebration of Christmas:

"There was a big open air midnight Mass – under the mango trees with a big full tropical moon."[223]

One can imagine being there: standing in the congregation with the cool night breeze washing away the stuffy heat of the day. The joyful celebration of the birth of Christ must have been a moment of rest and comfort to all present in the hard and fearful grip of war. His letters often enquire after the confrères and of course his brother Fr. William Bradley C.Ss.R., known as Bias. In February he was in Scapa Flow and so by March, having returned to the tropics was beginning to enjoy the climate a little more:

"I have been kept only moderately busy – just as well in a way as this is the hot season – a great and not unpleasant contrast to Scapa Flow – Feb!"[224]

A letter dated 1st April 1943 is mainly concerned with the various Redemptorists he has encountered recently: namely Fr. Smith and Fr. Simpson. What then follows is an account of the triumphant return of Fr. Simpson with his regiment to Durban:

"Fr. Simpson (whom I met in the guise of conquering hero returning from the wars.) I happened to be in Durban at the time: he marched with the troops through the town. As he was the only one with a Roman collar on people were shouting 'Bravo Padre'."[225]

The difficulties of censorship prevented Fr. Bradley from re-porting much of his news but in his final letter of 17th May 1943 he says: "You don't get much war news these days from these parts – let us hope things will wake up soon."[226] The climate and the lack of positive action combined with the constant threat of attack must have played on his mind. He does however note a terrifying example of dangers of life in the African bush: "a lion stole one of the sentries and ate him – which was unnecessary."[227] On 2nd July 1943 Fr. Bradley was aboard the *Hoihow*, travelling from Mauritius to begin his leave, when the vessel was torpedoed and sank. It took only two minutes for the ship to sink: 91 crew, 5 gunners and 100 passengers were lost. There were only four survivors of the event who managed to get into a raft and were picked up by the U.S. boat *Mormaciver* on the 8th July 1943 and landed in Monte Video on the 26th July of the same year. News came to Fr. Provincial from the Admiralty that Fr. Bradley was missing in action. The chronicles note:

"It should be recorded that earlier in the month Fr. Provincial received official intimation from the Admiralty that Fr. Thomas Bradley is missing since June last. He was chaplain in the navy – our oldest chaplain – and was at sea all during the 1914-1918 world war. We still hope he may have been rescued."[228]

On 1st June 1943 Fr. Provincial sent a copy of his Provincial letter to Fr. Bradley. It was the centenary year for the province and a matter for great celebration. In the letter he recalls the difficulties and dangers that Redemptorist missionaries face in bringing the Gospel to the nations and writes concerning the war:

"...we must pray; trusting unwaveringly, however dark the prospect, in Our Lady of Victories, who by her perpetual succour will bring her sons and her soldiers, bravely persevering through the storm of battle, to the promised triumph and the eternal peace of heaven."[229]

This letter calling for all to have courage in adversity and hope in the seemingly hopeless situation of the war never reached Fr. Bradley. The envelope is stamped 'return to sender' and the message printed underneath reads: "It is with the deepest regret you are informed that the addressee is missing presumed killed on active service"[230], although his death was not formally acknowledged by the Admiralty until 21st February 1944. Two letters from Fr. Provincial to Fr. Bradley were also never received. In them Fr. Bradley is requested by the Provincial to make a visitation of the South African province which had, due to the war, not had a visitation in some years. Sadly Fr. Bradley would not be able to carry out this work. Letters between the Provincial and the Admiralty and Fr. Bradley's family are frequent and full of hope that he may be found alive:

"Four survivors were picked up...These men say they saw three men on a raft and two clinging to an upturned boat. No news has been received of these other survivors."[231]

However this was not the case. Archbishop Leo of Mauritius reported that:

"Fr. Bradley had gone on two months' leave from Mombasa, and had said that he had wanted to go and see the men in Madagascar. He called in at Mauritius and spent a week with his Grace there. When he sailed...the ship was torpedoed two or three days out and a fortnight later four men in a raft turned up and told the tale of the loss of the ship and all hands except themselves."[232]

He had indeed perished at sea and soon arrangements began for the funeral: once the Admiralty had declared Fr. Bradley 'presumed killed'. Fr. Provincial wrote to the Admiralty to enquire what the proper procedure for a naval funeral was. Admiral Boyd wrote to say he would be glad to attend the requiem Mass. The Mass was set for 29th October 1943 at 11 am. Those present included the senior Royal Naval Chaplain Mgr. Dewey, Admiral Boyd and Commander Slattery. His brother Fr. William and his sister Miss Nora Bradley were present there to represent the family as Fr. Bradley's mother was not able to travel up from Falmouth for the service. Fr. Costello C.Ss.R. RN was the celebrant at the Mass and Fr. Prime C.Ss.R. preached. Fr. Prime said this of Fr. Bradley:

— ✠ —

Pray for the Eternal Repose of the soul of

REV. THOMAS BRADLEY, C.SS.R.,

Temporary Chaplain Royal Navy,

Who was killed by enemy action in the

Indian Ocean, on July 2nd, 1943,

At the age of 58, in the 34th year of his

Priesthood and the 39th year of his

Profession.

—✠—

We give Thee thanks, O Holy Lord, Father Almighty, through Jesus Christ Our Lord; for, through Him, the hope of a blessed resurrection hath shone forth to us, so that we who are saddened by the certainty of death may be consoled by the promise of eternal life to come. For to Thy faithful ones, O Lord, life is but changed, not taken away. And in exchange for this earthly home, an eternal one is prepared in the heavens. Therefore do we sing with the angelic choirs the hymn of Thy glory, evermore saying: Holy, Holy, Holy.—(*Preface, Requiem Mass*).

May he rest in peace.

Our Lady, Star of the Sea, pray for him.

"If we consider the man himself, the character which actuated all his exterior life, we can some it up in one word. He was a priest with a keen sense of a priest's duties and responsibilities."[233]

The senior naval chaplain wrote of him: "He was a good priest, beloved by all and loving the sea and sea-faring men. If he be dead, his end seems just such a one as he himself would have chosen."[234]

He was mourned by all within the congregation as:

"...a kindly, patient and gentle confrère. His life was austere and he was a man with a deep spirit of prayer; but austere though he was, his unfailing good humour and hilarity made him a treasure and a solace to all of those who, in his community, shared his life."[235]

Horatio Nelson himself declared: "I could not tread these perilous paths in safety, if I did not keep a saving sense of humour."[236] Fr. Bradley's ancestor Admiral Hardy stood beside Nelson on HMS *Victory* at the Battle of Trafalgar and so it seems fitting that this saving sense of humour he learned at the hand of the greatest naval commander in history was there for Fr. Bradley in dark times to help him through. In the navy he had been a "welcome messmate and friend"[237] and had brought solace to men in the most desperate situations. He had worked hard and had been willing to spend and be spent for God. In bringing to a close this remembrance of Fr. Bradley it has been a privilege to research his life and step into the history of so great and holy a man. Not holy as people often think of it, not a statue, but a man in touch with God who saw Christ in the faces of those to whom he ministered and a man who shone with the light of the Redeemer. His aim had been to be a true and holy Redemptorist and that aim he undoubtedly achieved.

May he rest in peace.

REV. FR. MARK GERARD COSTELLO C.SS.R. RN

Born	1913
Professed	1930
Ordained	1936
Died	2005

Father Gerard 'Gerry' Costello was born on 8th May 1913 at number 15 Nook Rise in Wavertree, Liverpool, to Mark Joseph and Mary Josephine Costello. His father, Mark Costello had served as a ship's steward and so the sea was always in his blood. The birth certificate names the new born child Mark Gerard but it seems that he was always known by his middle name Gerard during his long years as a Redemptorist. His education began at Our Lady's RC School in Wavertree. In September 1924, he entered St. Francis Xavier's College in Liverpool, which is now under the care of the De Lamennais Brothers and is situated very close by to the Redemptorist Monastery Church of Bishop Eton. During his school years he was in contact with Fr.

McCabe C.Ss.R. at Bishop Eton who kept a close eye on the progress of his studies. He seems to have got on well with Fr. McCabe and writes as though to a friend of many years:

"The holidays are on at present and I am enjoying myself in the nice hot days that we have had of late."[238]

On 20th July 1929, Fr. Gerry entered the Redemptorist Novitiate at Kinnoull, Perth, Scotland. He made his first profession on 15th August 1930 before moving to Hawkstone Hall in Shrewsbury to begin his studies for the sacred priesthood. His Prefect of Students wrote in January 1934:

"This student is doing extremely well...He was professed temporarily in 1930, and would have been finally professed in August 1933 except that he is underage."[239]

And again, in June 1934, Fr. Prefect writes:

"This student is maintaining in all ways his high level of spiritual and intellectual endeavour."[240]

His final profession was made in 1934 and he was ordained on 7th March 1936 in Birmingham at Erdington Abbey. However, because he was only 23 years of age at the time of his ordination, he required a dispensation to be ordained as the minimum age limit for ordination was 24. It was common at that time for Redemptorists to be ordained at the beginning of the fourth year of theological study, which for Fr. Gerry was one year too early, so Fr. Gerry had to remain a student until 1936 when he was granted permission to go forward for ordination.

Following his ordination he was appointed to the mission staff at Erdington Abbey for one year, after which he was sent to complete his 'second novitiate'. He returned to the mission staff at Erdington until 1938 when he was sent to Clapham to give missions out of the Redemptorist house of St. Mary's. With the outbreak of the Second World War in 1939 things began to change very quickly. A large number of the children from the area surrounding St. Mary's had to be evacuated and Fr. Gerry served as chaplain to the evacuees at St. Mary's West Hoathly, in Sussex. In May 1940, he joined the Royal Navy as a Chaplain and served until 1947.

Being able to follow his father to sea must have been very special and of course Fr. Gerry would have met Fr. Thomas Bradley C.Ss.R. R.N. during the years of peace between wars and heard stories of serving the poor and most abandoned at sea. Fighting to ensure that as many as possible might attend the sacraments was indeed a worthy ministry. However, it is essential to point out that none of these men chose to go, they were sent by the congregation, missioned to the forces. Following initial training Fr. Gerry served until 1941 with the Home Fleet Destroyers, after which he was moved to HMS Collingwood where he served as base Chaplain until 1944. The Chronicles note that in 1944 he was transferred to the Royal Marines: "a very dangerous posting."[241] Indeed, the Royal Marines, who are often described as Britain's elite fighting force, are regularly the first into the fray and the last to come away. It was during his service with the Royal Marines that the most astonishing acts of bravery, courage and humility come.

The United States of America entered the Second World War in 1943 following the attack on Pearl Harbour by Japan. The Allied Forces prepared for a large-scale operation which, if it was successful, would end the war by Christmas: Operation Market Garden. The plan was to drop huge numbers of men by parachute behind enemy lines. These men would then storm the bridges over the Rhine and would be reinforced by the main invasion force landing on the beaches of Normandy, known as Operation Neptune. In the end the mission did not achieve its aim but it only just fell short. Fr. Costello was chaplain to the 4th Special Service Brigade and landed on Juno beach in Normandy at 8:30 am with 48 Royal Marine Commandos, one of four units of commandos that formed the brigade. The Prime Minister, Winston Churchill announced over the wireless the following morning that the landings had taken place:

"An immense armada of upwards of 4,000 ships, together with several thousand smaller craft, crossed the English Channel. Massed airborne landings have been successfully effected behind the enemy lines."[242]

During the First World War Churchill had served as First Lord of the Admiralty and he never forgot the failure of the landings at Gallipoli, where thousands of men died because it took too long to land the troops, which gave the Turkish forces time to prepare to repel them. Churchill was sent back to the front line and served bravely but he never forgot the huge loss of life at Gallipoli.

On 5th June 2004, 60 years later, at the ripe old age of 91, Fr. Gerry gave an interview to Mian Ridge of the *Tablet* in which he described his experience of the D-Day landings. This was the first time that Fr. Costello took part in a battle:

"We passed the Isle of Wight and watched the coast of England fading away and wondered 'will I ever see this again?' None of us had slept very much on the way over but I remember waking up to this tremendous scene. There were ships and crafts of every size, as far as the eye could see."[243]

Shortly before the landings took place, a sergeant asked Fr. Costello to receive him into the church and that is what happened. Many years later the two men met again, the sergeant was now a priest himself. Before the marines were to land, the 3rd Canadian Division was to attempt to clear and secure Juno beach and make way for the commandos to assault the nearby German stronghold of Langrune-sur-Mer. However the Allies had certainly underestimated the preparedness of the German forces and when 48 Commando landed it was apparent that the fight for the beach was very much still underway:

"As we got nearer things began to get noisy...There was a lot of gunfire from the shore and one felt that one might be hit. Then, suddenly, it was time to jump down the ramp, into the sea, and make your way onto the beach. We jumped into quite a depth of water, not quite above the neck, but high, and stumbled ashore."[244]

The landing was made on a narrow strip of land, code named 'Nan Red' and this this spit of land was already congested with artillery and tanks before the arrival of the commandos. The fortification they had come to take from the Germans was raining down heavy fire upon everything and everyone who stepped on that beach and one cannot help but be moved by Fr. Gerry's recollection of the carnage of the D-Day landings:

"Everywhere there were broken-down and blown up tanks and people lying around; all sorts of indecent things..."[245]

However, walking in the very shadow of death Fr. Gerry was always aware of those in need. He came across a group of soldiers from the battered and bruised Canadian Division who were taking cover behind the sea wall. His first thought was to rally these men and to restore their hope:

"So I stopped and had a chat, to encourage them, and then I started to get off the beach."[246]

Arriving into that hellish scene must have been truly terrifying and it takes a brave man to remain calm under fire. It takes an especially brave man to go unarmed into that field of battle and provide succour to men who are close to breaking point. The chaplain for the Church of England had been wounded on the beach and Fr. Costello stopped to speak with him and to encourage him not to give up: "I had a word with him and encouraged him..."[247] Indeed, Fr. Gerry was the only Chaplain in his brigade to make it through the landings uninjured and so for a time he was there alone serving all:

"For a while I was trying to look after everyone; they were most welcome..."[248]

As he made his way off the beach he gave the last rites to a number of soldiers who lay dying and comforted the men as they passed away. One officer had just witnessed four of his men being blown up. The "shell-shocked officer" was "deeply distressed" and so Fr. Costello remained with him for a moment to calm his nerve so that he could continue to lead his troops[249]. At the end of day around half of the commandos that had landed had been killed. Such huge losses must have been a massive shock and yet Fr. Gerry had to be strong for the men who were his parishioners. The Holy Sacrifice of the Mass was celebrated in the "sacristy of a wrecked local church"[250]. Fr. Gerry's batman, a soldier assigned to the chaplain to assist him, arrived with his jeep, which left him free to assist the troops and offer his services where jobs needed to be done so that marines needn't be taken away from their current task. He came across an injured officer and drove him back to the hospital, which had been set up on the beach:

"We had to cross a vast field where a lot of landmines had been blown up, so it was very bumpy, very hard going...The officer was in terrible agony and he cried out every time the jeep shook. It was a terrible journey and it took ages. But I got him to the beach dressing station and left him there. I learnt later that he had died during the night."[251]

That night must have been a terrible one. The men must have been exhausted, emotionally drained and concerned for what was to come next. Fr. Costello was billeted in the Parish Priest's outhouse and slept on the cold, hard, stone floor:

"No one got much sleep because we kept hearing that the enemy was approaching."[252]

It was in fact a unit of German Panzer Tanks that was heading in their direction.

In the following days, the Allies made their way forward, taking one village after another. Fr. Gerry generally followed on foot ministering to the wounded and helping wherever he was needed. Occasionally he was able to get a lift with armoured vehicles and recalls one incident when he quite literally dodged a bullet:

"I remember catching a lift into one village; I sat on a trailer full of weapons…As we drove into the village there was a lovely promenade of shops, but what wasn't so nice was a sniper, who started firing, particularly at me because I was on top of this trailer. So I jumped off and ran, and as I passed the shops the bullets went into the lovely glass in a long line."[253]

In one instant Fr. Costello was asked to locate the graves of two from 41 Royal Marine Commandos and set off to meet the priest. The priest made him "recite the Hail Mary in French to prove his identity."[254] Credentials established, the priest helped Fr. Gerry to find the two men:

"Then he helped me find the graves, and I marked their location as carefully as I could on my map and went back."[255]

The Marines moved further into Normandy and away from the coast but progress was slow. Brigadier Leicester, the Brigade Commander, asked Fr. Gerry to say Mass in a small town in no-man's land called Sallanelles, where there was no parish priest. Fr. Costello called the Brigadier, "my good Catholic Brigadier "[256].

"We couldn't go by road, it was mined. So myself and my batman, who had by this point arrived with my jeep, crawled into Sallanelles twice a week to say Mass. The church was always full."[257]

However no-man's land was always a dangerous place to be and eventually they came under heavy fire:

"One day the Germans started to shell the town in the middle of Mass and I remember bringing the children up around the altar to look after them."[258]

His faithful batman remained his friend after the war and the two were regularly in touch:

"He was good and kind to me during the war and has been ever since…He's getting old now, poor fellow, like me."[259]

It is hard to imagine today, a Redemptorist priest being followed around by his batman and yet in the field of battle it must have been a great comfort to know that he was not alone and could rely on this man to help him get to those who needed his care. I find the image vaguely reminiscent of Simon of Cyrene helping Christ to bear his cross. Fr. Costello was essentially alone in every respect: he had no other chaplains around him; rarely the company of other priests; he had to be strong for the men and could not impose his own problems on them and he was left alone to arrange the spiritual care of the men in his brigade while enduring the same danger and fear as every other member of that brigade. His batman was the one confident he had, the one man whose purpose it was to assist him: he could trust this man.

As the Allied forces strengthened their position and began to press on Fr. Costello together with his batman entered a town to a rapturous welcome from its Mayor:

"I remember crossing the Seine and going into this town and

getting the most terrific welcome from the mayor and crowds of people...The troops came later but we were the first there. That night, a family offered me a room and that was the first bed I had slept in for three months. Marvellous."[260]

The mayor encouraged Fr. Costello to pursue the Germans who were retreating on the other side of the village, but as they were the first men to arrive and were alone, they declined the proposal. In November 1944, he took part in 'Operation Infatuate', another Anglo-Canadian effort, which was launched to allow Allied shipping to enter the Port of Antwerp in order to ease the problems concerning the stretched supply lines. In 1945, he was posted to the Royal Navy's training establishment at HMS *Raleigh*, where he served until 1947. He received official notice of his release from service on 21st July 1947 with the date set for him to leave the navy on 17th September 1947. This notification was accompanied by a sharp reminder of the Official Secrets Act and it seems he took that very seriously, not many of the confrères knew much more than that he had served as a chaplain and had been present at D-Day.

After his time in the Royal Navy and with the Royal Marines he returned to the London Province and was posted to Hawkstone Hall to become the Prefect of Students and remained there for three years and indeed some of the community present in St. Mary's Clapham today had Fr. Costello as their Prefect.

While in this post he re-introduced printing and book binding as a hobby for the students. It was during this time at Hawkstone that he wrote a letter to his "good Catholic Brigadier" who responded in a letter dated 28th April. In the letter, Brigadier Leicester congratulates Fr. Gerry on his new posting, saying:

"Teaching or, rather I imagine, controlling and guiding students must be extremely interesting." [261]

I am sure his experience of dealing with men who lived under extremely high pressure stood him in good stead for heading the studendate. The memory of the men who were lost, as one would expect, was never far from their minds:

"I am sure that sometimes you say Mass for the dead of 4 Commando Brigade."[262]

The Brigadier was posted to America following the war and writes of his experience of the American way of life:

"Quite apart from their Prosperity (with a big P) this rather volatile and if I may say so, wooden-headed nation is thoroughly enjoying being the most powerful country in the world."[263]

Aside from the tongue in cheek descriptions of his hosts there is the feeling of the ending of an era about this letter. Two men who stood side-by-side in the face of terrible danger, now reminiscing about those days. The days of the British Empire were numbered and that feeling seems to have made its way across the Atlantic:

"They are most sympathetic and pro-English but quite convinced of the decay of the British Empire, at the same time being resolved that no American Empire will take its place and responsibilities."[264]

Brigadier Leicester goes on to describe the wonderful freedom he has experienced since arriving in America:

"I have travelled quite a lot on both the east and west coasts." It is refreshing after the tight controls of England to find what a large measure of independence each state has."[265]

Freedoms returned slowly but steadily in Britain and bit by bit rationing was ended. His work at the House of studies in Hawkstone was highly important however, if he thought his wandering days were over, he was wrong and he certainly moved about a lot.

In 1950 Fr. Costello was moved to Perth where he became novice master but only for one year.

His next move was a move home to Liverpool and to Bishop Eton for a further year until he returned to join the 'Travelling Mission' based out of Hawkstone Hall.

In 1953 Fr. Gerry moved to Sunderland to the community of St. Benet's to join the mission team and was there for the next four years. In 1957 he was appointed Provincial Procurator and was posted to Clapham until 1969: his first period of real stability for some time, although during 1959-1960 he lived in the Redemptorist community at Liguori in Missouri, USA to research the way the American Redemptorist Publishing arm was run. From 69 to 72 he was Rector, superior, of the community in Plymouth and was also the Parish Priest. In 1972, he was appointed to the same positions in Sunderland at St. Benet's. In 1975, Fr. Costello was sent to the community at Machnylleth, in Wales, again in the same positions. After a brief spell at Bishop Eton Fr. Costello made what was to be his final move to Chawton, where Redemptorist Publications can now be found. In his documents, he refers to himself as the 'anchor man' of the community and indeed one brother mischievously referred to him as the 'lord of the manor'. He never lost his love of the traditions he had picked up in the armed forces and seems to have considered the refectory as the wardroom, a number of confreres quote him as saying: "We don't do that in the mess."

Far from being a stuffy character Fr Costello seems to have been a humble and grateful man, two qualities that enable us to live life for God without anxiety and in freedom and generosity of heart. Responding to a letter from the Provincial congratulating him on the celebration of his platinum jubilee of the profession of his vows as a Redemptorist, he says:

"I am truly grateful for your goodness to me. I likewise appreciate the care and friendship of so many confrères down the years. I can only repay this by my prayers."[266]

Fr. Gerry became increasingly unwell and he passed away at the age of 92 in a hospital run by the Daughters of the Cross at Hazelmere. It seems fitting to end this account of the life of such a man of service, a man whose whole life was dedicated to his priesthood within the congregation, with the words of the Superior General of the Congregation of the Most Holy Redeemer. Most Rev. Fr. Juan M. Lasso de la Vega C.Ss.R. wrote to Fr. Gerry regarding his recent Golden Jubilee of Priesthood in a letter dated 6th February 1986, saying:

"I send you this greeting not only in my own name but in the name of the whole Congregation. For the Congregation is proud of you because of the service you have given the church and the example you have given the confrères. All appreciated the grateful way in which you performed so many diverse services: war time military chaplain, Prefect of Students, and Provincial Bursar. But your mediating grace to so many souls through personal contact is recorded only in the Lord's book of your priesthood."[267]

REV. FR. CHARLES WATSON C.SS.R. C.F.

Born 1867

Professed 1891

Ordained 1897

Died 1918

Fr. Watson was born on the 26th August 1867. He was a sensitive soul and to understand how he came to live his life it is important to understand where he came from. His father, who was born in Glasgow to a Protestant family, had been well travelled and had lived in Belgium for some years before purchasing a property from an Englishman in the Belgian municipality of Gedinne in the Province of Namur, near to the French boarder. Fr. Watson's father enlarged the property to establish a small farm, finding "a good honest man"[268] to work the farm for him. Watson Sr. fell in love with the farmer's daughter, who was "tall and nice looking, promising piety and simplicity"[269], and wasted no time in securing her hand in marriage despite the laughter of his friends who no doubt felt he had married below his station. Fr. Watson's feelings regarding his father's decision to marry for love is quite clear:

"How wonderful the ways of Providence! Who would have thought, when he made such a foolish marriage according to the opinion of the world, that the poor peasant girls would prove his guardian angel through life, would save the rest of a fortune fast going to ruin, would bring up in the most Christian manner five children and have the happiness to see her husband die a Catholic and two of her children consecrating themselves to God, one as a Little Sister of the Poor and the other as a Redemptorist."[270]

Written in his own immaculate handwriting the formative years Fr. Charles spent in Belgium sound like something from a fairy tale. He describes the immense freedom he and his siblings had in their isolated home in the middle of the woods: "we could go wherever we liked and do whatever we liked."[271] He was the eldest son with only one sister his senior. At the age of seven the family obtained a governess to come and teach the children as the school in the village was too far away. At the age of eleven Fr. Charles made his first Holy Communion, which he said: "left in me very vivid recollections even to the present time."[272] Receiving Holy Communion is often taken for granted these days as part of the course of Christian life but this was not the case for Fr. Watson who had waited patiently for his turn to receive Christ in the Eucharist:

"When I used to see the happy rows of girls all dressed in white and the boys in black approaching the Holy Table I often found myself yearning to do the same and I was even moved to tears."[273]

He had been prepared for his first Holy Communion by his governess and she was obviously a woman of strong faith because young Charles was profoundly moved by the experience:

"On the day of communion I was greatly moved and was really well aware of the importance of the act I was going to perform; before Mass I went and threw myself at the knees of my parents and governess and begged their pardon for all the faults I had committed against them: During the Mass I prayed very fervently especially after communion in which I tasted the sweetness of the presence of Our Lord."[274]

Soon after this the family moved and Charles began to attend a local school where he was badly bullied for attending communion. His parents learning of this abuse sent him as a day scholar to St. Louis School, which was run by priests and where Charles excelled. He eventually entered the Jesuit College in 1881 but seems to have run out of steam academically. Later that year he suffered a terrible blow, his father died at the age of 53. He had been unwell for some time but his death was a terrible shock for Charles:

"Wonderful to relate three priests, friends of his, came quite by accident at his deathbed and had the pleasure to hear him give answers to all the questions they thought fit to ask him and we had the happiness to see him buried with the rites of the Catholic Church."[275]

With his father gone some relatives in England wrote to Charles' mother and offered to send him to a school at their own expense. Charles began to study at Ushaw College in Durham, where he remained for four years, which he said: "were happy years and they had a very great influence on the whole of my life."[276] During his time at the Jesuit College at home in Belgium Charles had fallen in with the wrong group and he obviously felt the move to Ushaw helped him to get back to his old self: "I was recalled to a firm and manly virtue."[277] At the request of his English relatives Charles now explored several avenues of life he might choose including becoming an engineer and a doctor. However he describes the moment at Ushaw, when before the statue of Our Lady he asked her what he should do:

"As I was praying fervently before a beautiful statue of Our Lady, like I used to do every day in order to know what situation I ought to choose amongst those that had been put before me, the idea that perhaps I ought to be a priest came into my head and I may safely say that since that time, that is to say since 1884, that idea never left me and it followed me even through all those different paths of life I followed afterwards and even in spite of my effort to put it away from me…"[278]

Having returned to Belgium to his rural home Charles found it very difficult to maintain his studies, despite the kind offer of a local priest to tutor him. Eventually Charles secured a good and able teacher and found a confessor who he hoped would help him: "clear the doubts which had been troubling me for two years and which prevented me from getting decided on the way I should direct my studies."[279] This hope was short lived however as the man he had chosen to be his confessor said that he hoped to see him soon at the seminary: this seemingly innocuous statement set off a chain of thought in Charles' head that lead to him leaving this man and not securing another confessor for some time. At this stage in his life Fr. Charles seems to go through a crisis of faith: he rarely went to confession and gave little time to his studies, which eventually led to his teacher ending their lessons. Charles was sent to the 'Little Seminary' but admits that his work was poor and his mind elsewhere. It was there that he met a young American who was studying French at the college and as Charles was the only student who could speak English they soon became firm friends. For Charles' this man seemed "very daring and worldly"[280] and it must have felt like a breath of fresh air had blown in a reminder of those sweet days of his innocence playing in the woods surrounding his home. These two found their entertainment in playing tricks and pranks. Indeed, in a scene reminiscent of a William Brown novel, one day after being out in the town and staying all night the two were called in to the master's office who reprimanded them strongly:

"As he was young and very excitable, instead of listening he got into a temper and gave us a good specimen of a strong lecture calling us men without morals etc. etc."[281]

The two reprobates were suspended for a week! Charles had made a choice to live according to his desires showing a lack of gratitude for the many graces he had received in his life. He heard the voice of the Lord telling him to repent and come back but tuned it out. One is reminded of the three denials of St. Peter, who considered himself Christs most loyal disciple and would never abandon him and yet he did, three times. For the first time in his life Charles seems to have put Christ, whom he felt he would never abandon on the day of his first Holy Communion, out of his life: like so many of us there would be other moments in his life when Charles turned his back on Christ and yet although the flame of his faith flickered it never went out. This experience gave Charles a nudge in the right direction. He had heard that he might not be accepted back into the seminary and decided to avoid the humiliation and instead get his life in order. He once again sought out a priest who would tutor him in private and found just such a man in a remote part of the Province of Luxembourg. He remained in the region, which was famous for its wild and picturesque scenery, for around eight months until Easter 1888. This time was some of the happiest he spent and in his long walks through the mountainous countryside he found a way to return to a well-balanced, regulated life directed towards God:

"During that time, I became very pious and used to draw great joys from communion and again my ideas of becoming a priest came back to me with greater force than ever."[282]

Eventually Charles grew tired of his life again and found every excuse to abandon it for a more pleasing existence elsewhere. Just at that time he received an invitation to join a friend who was studying some distance away near his home. Charles spent a lot of time in prayer but, as so many of us do, he realised that he was praying with the intention of obtaining what pleased him most. It seems to have been both literally and figuratively and uphill struggle for Charles to leave his situation in the mountains:

"I left Dinez with a heavy heart and with the strong conviction that I was doing wrong. The conviction was so strong that as

I was climbing the mountain opposite the one where the little church and the house of the priest were standing all alone I turned around, sat down and fell into a long and sad silence. The happiness and purity of the life I had been leading struck me in a very forcible manner, I heard voices within me telling me to go back, the future life I was to lead would be perhaps brighter, but would it be better? Such was the question that was in my head. With great effort I stifled my feelings and went on my way and as I had about ten miles to walk before I reached the station many a time on the way did I feel the remorse of conscience and the voices telling me to go back but I bid them be silent and I consider this as one of the big faults of my life."[283]

Charles had denied Christ for the second time. At Linchamps, in the Ardennes, life was certainly less strict but Charles found it a trying experience. The people were not religious and once again he was challenged about his faith, even by his friends. He stood his ground for the first time and gave witness to Christ and soon felt his faith had been strengthened as was his fortitude:

"In order to practice religious duties openly where human respect is the general law by which everybody is guided no small amount of courage was to be put forward."[284]

Soon after his arrival his friend travelled to Paris to sit his examinations for bachelor of art. He passed but stayed in Paris and lost the faith. Charles seems sad as he relates this event: "He lost the faith as I often told him he would do; the last that I heard of him was that more sensible ideas were coming back to him."[285] Once again Charles found himself alone and without direction. He could not settle on his vocation and at this stage we, who have the benefit of hindsight, wonder what he was waiting for. Denis McBride, in his book 'Journeying with Jonah', describes the crisis of identity, outlook and direction. In other words, 'who am I?', 'where am I going?' and 'what guides my discernment?' Charles had felt several times the call to become a priest, but something held him back. He could not see where he was going. Maybe his outlook was still guided by the world, by what would be the most comfortable path, not necessarily the right path. He was sent to make his retreat at the Jesuit novitiate near Gent and while there made the decision that he would study for one more year and return to discern his future. He went to the seminary at Bastogne to study Philosophy and although his studies were not a success he made considerable ground in his spiritual life. He received communion regularly and read pious works including the 'Imitation of Christ' and soon he felt able to make a very important decision:

"Towards Easter after many fervent prayers, novenas to Our Lady and communions made with the intention of knowing what I should do, my mind had grown much firmer and I at least decided to quit the world, a thing which up to that time I had not yet done and I felt myself distinctly called to the religious state of the foreign missions."[286]

Charles once again decided to move on and return to Dinez to study privately once more. He was strongly advised not to follow this course but decided once again to insist the voice of his conscience hold its tongue and went on his way. In Dinez, while riding his bicycle over the mountains in the dark, Charles fell while travelling at speed down-hill and struck his head hard. He was unconscious for a good while and was eventually found and carried home, where he remained in bed for several days. His body was battered and broken but eventually he got up the courage to ask for a mirror:

"I could not help shivering when I saw the ugly wound verging on close to the temple and I saw that it was nothing less than a miracle that I had not been killed."[287]

When this period of convalescence was ended, he returned to Bastogne to the seminary but found he had fallen behind and felt unable to catch up. It was then that he received a letter from his second sister:

in which she was telling me of her decision of quitting the world and joining the Little Sisters of the Poor, after she had made a good retreat and been under the direction of Father Jacobs C.Ss.R....I wrote her immediately a letter of congratulations telling her that I would also like to see Father Jacobs in order to see whether he could do something for me."[288]

On his sisters' advice he attended, with her letter of introduction, the mission Fr. Jacobs was preaching at a near-by church on the 6th December. He heard for the first time of the blessed title of Our Lady of Perpetual Succour, who he was told was the patron of desperate cases and abandoned sinners:

"I was quite struck with new thoughts and I exclaimed 'Well my mother I also am a desperate case so you are bound to help me and let me do what God wants of me' and from that day I prayed to Our Lady of Perpetual Succour."[289]

Indeed, not long before Charles attended the mission his mother had joined the newly established Confraternity of Our Lady of Perpetual Succour, a fact which certainly had some bearing on his future. Fr. Jacobs was well known for helping people to discern their vocations. Charles arrived at the mission but had only half an hour to speak to Fr. Jacobs but this he said:

"was enough for the designs of God...When we met I gave him a brief outline of my life and he asked me a lot of questions, then after a short time of reflection he said 'Yes, yes, you must become a Redemptorist, join the English Province and go and present yourself at Clapham at Easter, meanwhile be faithful to that idea alone. Follow my advice and during Holy Week come and make a retreat with me."[290]

The bluntness of this conversation rather startled poor Charles but Fr. Jacobs saw in this man a great love of God and a true devotion to Our Lady of Perpetual Succour. He also surely saw a weak soul who given the chance could become a perpetual discerner, but Christ came to call the weak did he not? Fr. Jacobs seems to have been a wise man and indeed he solved Charles' identity crisis: he could now answer the three questions mentioned earlier. Who was he? He was a Redemptorist. Where was he going? He was going to offer his life in service of God in the English Province. Finally, what governed his life? At last he could say God's will. Despite his shock at the speed of the decision, Charles went away content:

"I felt as if this time at last I must give way without discussion and all the objections and ideas that I had prepared were completely forgotten and when I went away I felt so glad and so happy that I could not explain what had come over me."[291]

Charles went to make his retreat with Fr. Jacobs and felt confirmed in his vocation. However, there was to be one more wobble in Charles' path towards God: Fr. Jacobs had set a time to hear his general confession but Charles was late:

"Being not prepared at that time on account of scruples and negligence I only went to him half an hour later than the fixed time. Father Jacobs had been waiting for me and so was or seemed to be in a temper, he gave me a strong lecture; I stood silent, surprised to hear such a lecture for a fault which seemed to me so little and when he saw me thus he said that I should have fallen on my knees to beg his pardon, that I was proud good for nothing and said he had nothing more to do with me and sent me back to my room and said he would think over what he should do."[292]

Fr. Jacobs does sound a fearsome character and yet he had a point. Charles admitted that his negligence contributed to his late arrival and we must remember the awesome nature of the sacrament of reconciliation. It is nothing less than the sovereign grace of God by which we are absolved, made clean again. This is a matter of supreme importance and deserves to be taken seriously and perhaps that was Fr. Jacobs point: how can you bring plentiful redemption to the world as Gods Redemptorist if you don't think it important yourself? However, we must also remember that Charles is a sensitive character and his scruples may well have delayed his going to confession. His state of mind following this dressing down was certainly not a peaceful one:

"When I went back to my room I was in a terrible state of mind but I had the good inspiration to say some fervent prayers to Our Lady of Perpetual Succour, St Joseph and Blessed Clement whose picture was in my room and I put the whole thing in their hands."[293]

What followed brings to mind the 'agony in the garden': Charles paced the garden at once sad at once in a rage at the injustice of the whole thing. After some time, Fr. Jacobs joined him in the garden and I find significance in the words Fr. Charles used to describe this: "Father Jacobs came to walk with me in the garden." Is that not what we ask Our Lord to do each day in the turbulence of modern life? Charles explained what had happened and Fr. Jacobs heard his confession:

"He then went with me to my room and there I made a general confession; when I had finished, I felt such a great relief and peace of mind that when Father Jacobs embraced me at the end of the confession tears came rushing forth to my eyes and I wept like a child and from that time to the end of the retreat on Easter Sunday I enjoyed great consolations."[294]

At the conclusion of the retreat both men wrote letters to Fr. Provincial in the English Province and requested that Charles be granted admission. A letter came shortly after Easter asking him to travel to London to meet with Fr. Provincial and he immediately set off for London.

He was accepted without hesitation and felt true gratitude as we see in his own words:

"I consider this as of the great signs of my loving God's will in favouring this order of the Redemptorists for I could not help noticing it I had quite expected to be refused and I felt, in the lower part at least of the mind, a great disappointment when I saw myself received."[295]

He was a man truly blessed and in those last few weeks before he entered he needed God's grace to overcome the very real fear, temptation and sadness that leaving one way of life and taking up another brings with it and yet he felt again confirmed in his vocation:

"Those last struggles showed me and proved me the reality of my vocation; the temptations were so strong and the parting with friends, parents and native country was so painful that I felt clearly the special help given me by God for of myself I could not have gone through so much suffering without giving way."[296]

Having managed through all that time to hold back his emotions for the benefit of others he finally broke down while taking a last look around his family home, where he had been born and where he had enjoyed so much happiness with his family over the years:

"I cried like a child. I then threw myself into the arms of my poor sobbing mother and we remained thus closely embraced; I had not the strength to disengage myself but she full of courage did so and said 'My son, it is time, go where God calls you' then she fell back on the bench close by, her convulsions of sobs showing the immense sacrifice her mother's heart was making."[297]

At the station, he once again had to bid farewell to his friends and to his sister. He offered this pain to God in penance for his sins and boarded the train, where upon he was carried away as the world became less and less familiar to him and the pain eventually began to subside: "the last struggle had been hard but I was conquered; the sacrifice was accomplished, and well accomplished."[298]

He first visited his sister who was now a postulant with the Little Sisters of the Poor and who: "looked very happy and cheerful, already rewarded for the numerous sacrifices she had also made."[299] After some time in Brussel's he made the crossing from Ostend to Dover and it seems that after the pain and suffering of the parting of ways he finally found some small part of the clarity for which he had searched his entire life:

"I made the passage from Ostend to Dover, it was by a beautiful moonlight and I remained on deck the greatest part of the night; as I sat motionless between sky and water looking at the lights of Ostend disappearing in the distance, the whole of my life passed before my eyes, I saw the mistakes and I learned the lessons."[300]

After a few days spent in Clapham he travelled north to Liverpool to Bishop Eton where he was warmly received and: "soon was well rewarded for all my sufferings and troubles by that peace of mind which can only be found amongst the servants of God."[301]

Br. Charles Watson as he was now, was a man aware of his unsteady character but a man of real faith whose only hope was to, with the help of St. Alphonsus and Our Lady of Perpetual Succour, persevere until the end as a Redemptorist. He entered the novitiate and one year and one day later was professed in 1881. After six years' studies, he made final vows and was Ordained to the Sacred Priesthood.

Britain entered the First World War following the invasion of Belgium by the German armed forces and this must have been a great concern for Fr. Watson, whose family and friends still lived there. He was sent by Fr. Provincial to become a chaplain to the armed forces and served with the Army. The first mention of Fr. Watson with regard to the provision of chaplains to the armed forces comes on 19th February 1916 when he left his community at Bishop Eton in Liverpool to make his way to the front in France. He arrived in Clapham on 21st of the same month to continue his preparations. Two years into the war he was probably quite nervous and the Chronicles make the interesting side note that he was: "going to the front for the first time."[302] In the end, he was not alone as he departed Clapham for the front: he travelled with Fr. Howard who was also heading out to join the troops.

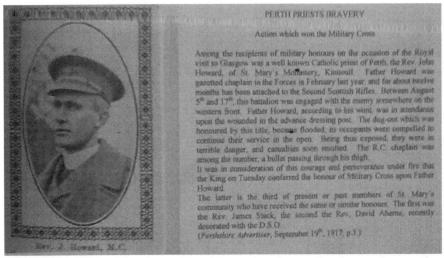

On 18th November Fr. Watson arrived at Clapham from the front in France and travelled on to Bristol before heading back to Bishop Eton where he arrived on 20th November: "Fr. Watson arrived today for a few days leave. He had many interesting things to tell about life at the front."[303] We know that Fr. Watson served in Egypt and from there served in Mesopotamia, modern day Iraq, where on 17th March 1917 the chronicles note that: "The British captured Bagdad last week."[304] The next news we have of Fr. Watson is a letter, received on 1st May 1917, informing the community at Bishop Eton that the troop transport ship he was on had been sunk near Malta. Unlike many of the fathers who served as chaplains, Fr. Watson does not seem to return to England very often at all and is barely mentioned in the chronicles. One can only assume that he was at his post in the Middle East serving those in his care. In the chronicles of Bishop Eton monastery on the 26th July 1918 we read: "News comes of the death of Fr. Watson C.F. in Mesopotamia. The nature of his death is not yet known."[305] In St. Mary's Clapham the chronicler writes:

"At dinner today V.R.F. Boyle read a telegram from Bagdad to say that Father Watson C.Ss.R. C.F. died on the 22nd of this month, fortified by the sacraments R.I.P."[306]

A solemn requiem was said for poor Fr. Watson. News soon arrived concerning the circumstances of Fr. Watsons passing. Fr. Watson's sister wrote to the community at Bishop Eton concerning Fr. Watson's death, she said:

"I have lately received a letter from the Father who assisted Fr. Watson in his last moments. His letter is consoling as it tells me that my poor brother had a peaceful death and that everything was done to save him. He was taken to the hospital on July 16th as he had fainted after his Mass, but he got immediately better. However two days after, a change for the worse came on and he became unconscious. The Father never left him for 24 hours hoping for a last message, but he only opened his eyes while he was being given the Last Sacraments – he smiled faintly as they rested on the priest's stole. He died at 8.30 a.m. on July 22nd and was buried the same morning with full military honours on the banks of the Euphrates. Fr. Deeley speaks about the good opinion that all who knew him had of my brother."[307]

Fr. P. Deeley C.F. was with Fr. Watson when he died and had remained with him since his condition turned critical. He sent a letter to Fr. Provincial in Clapham and included the letter for Fr. Watson's family. His account is truly moving:

"Watson was admitted to hospital on July 16th suffering from heat stroke. From what I gather he had been rather unwell for some days previously: he fainted on Sunday July 14th after Mass and I think also on one other day. He appears to have felt the great heat very much. After being taken to hospital he got much better and his condition gave no cause for anxiety. He improved each day and on the evening of July 19th (Friday) he was talking quite cheerfully to the Matron. During that night a sudden change for the worse took place and quite early on Saturday morning: July 20th he lost the power of speech and became unconscious. The hospital authorities immediately wired for the nearest priest. I came at once from Basra and by travelling all night I reached here at 8.30 a.m. on Sunday 21st. I went straight to him: he was quite unconscious. I gave him conditional absolution, extreme unction and the last blessing. I got a bed in the hospital and was with him constantly until he died peacefully at 8.30 a.m. July 22nd. He never recovered consciousness. But while I was anointing him, his eyes which were half closed, opened wide and looking at my stole he seemed to give just the faintest smile. I think he realized that I was a priest and that I was giving him the last rites. The doctors and nurses did everything possible to save him: but he never rallied after the 20th. He was buried with full military honours on the evening of July 22nd. During his short period of service in Mesopotamia he was stationed at Nasiriyah where he died and is buried. Nasiriyah is a town on the banks of the Euphrates about 120 miles from

Basra...Fr. Watson was loved and respected by all who came into contact with him. I should imagine that suffered from this terrible climate. But he was always brave and patient and zealous in the performance of his duties. He died as he lived, a good priest."[308]

He is buried in the Nasiriyah Cemetery of the Mesopotamia Expeditionary Force, his cross read: "Pray for the soul of Revd Charles Watson C.Ss.R. who died at Nasiriyah. July 22nd 1918. R.I.P."[309] He died far from the mountains and woodland of home but I think this he would be pleased. He had fulfilled his earnest wish as a young man: "but I hope with the help of St. Alphonsus and Our Lady of Perpetual Succour who brought me in this order of the Redemptorists to be able to persevere in it unto the end."[310] As to his personal effects, most were sent home to his next of kin, but Fr. Deeley kept his Mass kit, rosary, cross and relics promising to return them at the end of the war. After hostilities ceased he wrote to Fr. Provincial on 2nd December 1918 to explain that he had given the crucifix, rosary, relics and pyx to Fr. Farrell who promised to bring them back to Clapham. Fr. Watson's sister requested his rosary and crucifix and Fr. Deeley kept the Mass kit: "which has been very useful as one of the chaplains lost his in the Tigris."[311] One final reminder of the difficulties of being a chaplain at the front. Fr. Watson was a sensitive soul but a brave man who was not afraid to face his own personal demons head on and to grow into the man God made him to be. In his life, sadly cut short, he experienced to the fullest the beauty of this world and sacrificed everything to ensure that he was free for God to go wherever he was needed at the drop of a hat. It seems fitting somehow to end his account with the prayer of St. Alphonsus to the Blessed Sacrament, which contains an act of faith, an act of hope, an act of contrition and then the abandonment of oneself to God and to His will:

My Lord Jesus Christ, who, for the love you have for us, remain night and day in this Sacrament, full of compassion and love, awaiting, calling and welcoming all who come to visit you, I believe you are present in the Sacrament of the Altar. I adore you from the depth of my nothingness, and I thank you for all the graces you have bestowed upon me, especially for having given me yourself in this Sacrament, for having given me your most holy Mother Mary as my advocate and for having called me to visit you in this church. My Jesus, I love you with all my heart. I am sorry for having offended your infinite Goodness. I am resolved never more to offend you for the time to come, and now, although unworthy, I give myself completely to you. I renounce my own will, my affections, my desires and all that I possess. From now onwards do you dispose of me, and all that I have, as you please. All I ask of you is your holy love, final perseverance and the perfect fulfilment of your will. AMEN.

Our Lady of Perpetual Succour.

Pray for us.

St. Alphonsus and all our Redemptorist saints.

Pray for us.

REV. FR. BERNARD KAVANAGH C.SS.R. C.F.

Born 1864

Professed 1883

Ordained 1890

Died 1917

While at Bishop Eton in Liverpool Bernard Kavanagh, a Redemptorist Novice, wrote down his vocation story: "The more easily to discover and describe the causes which led to my vocation to the Congregation of the Most Holy Redeemer..."[312] He decided to divide his life thus far into four sections, the first of which being his life until the age of five. His father was born on the family estates in Carlow, in the South East of Ireland. The family had become poor through a combination of factors, most notably a series of failed business ventures and the "fines and confiscations of penal times"[313]. It seems life was very tough for the family: being Catholic excluded them from attending many schools meaning education was largely carried out by Fr. Kavanagh's grandfather who was a classical scholar. When he had done all he could for his family he sent them across the Atlantic to seek their fortune. Francis, the eldest, went to the United States, while Henry the second son was sent to Canada where he acquired a government posting. Henry went on to purchase some land but moved on to Montreal leaving the land in the care of the next brother Joseph. Of the four brothers only Bernard, Fr. Kavanagh's father, settled in Ireland before travelling to Paris to train as a Doctor. He found great success in Paris and fell in love with the city and the people. He went to the University to study for his M.D. degree and it was only a short while before he came to prominence by winning the "Stethescopic Prize"[314], which was the highest professional award attainable in Ireland at the time. This success caught the eye of one of Irelands leading physicians Sir William Wilde, father of Oscar Wilde, who wrote to Dr. Kavanagh and invited him to become his assistant. After a wonderful career with Sir William, Bernard was offered the post of resident Doctor at a hospital in Limerick and accepted the post. Sir William was sorry to see him go but often visited the family in Limerick, calling Dr. Kavanagh: "My dear boy, Bernard."[315] Fr. Kavanagh's mother was the last member of her family and so inherited "all that remained of the property of the Lynches in and about Limerick."[316] The family was now financially secure however for Dr. Kavanagh, all that this meant was that he could now devote much of his time free of charge to the poor. Indeed, he seems to have worked hard for the poor without ever seeking praise and his final words were: "Thank God I leave no debts behind me; but above all I thank Him that I have never taken anything from His Church or His Poor."[317] Fr. Kavanagh was born in Limerick, Ireland, on the 7th November 1864 and was one of six children, having four older sisters and one younger brother. Bernard's older sister was brought in to see him after he had been born recalled her first impressions:

"What at once attracted my attention was that he had a red mark on each temple. I asked who had hurt him. Someone answered that perhaps it was the Angel who had carried him down from Heaven. Child-like, I wanted to know all the details, and promptly asked how it had happened. Someone, I do not know who, lifted me up and showed me some chimney-pots on the other side of the street, distinctly pointing out the special one against which the accident had happened. All the "grown-ups" in the room seemed amused, and one of the exclaimed "How very carless"."[318]

This came in handy as an excuse later when being scalded for being a carless girl, she was able to reply: "Angels are carless too."[319] The children's nurse, Bridget O'Callaghan, had a great devotion to the "Holy Fathers"[320], the Redemptorists and spent most of her free time in the Redemptorist church. This certainly had an influence on young Bernard. She would attend the Holy Sacrifice of the Mass and then come back to repeat the sermon to the children for their benefit and often predicted that one-day Bernard would become a priest. Bridgett was devoted to young Bernard and: "All the love of her big grateful heart was lavished on him."[321] However, tempting it may have been to play on her favouritism, Bernard remained a humble soul and never took advantage of his gentle nurse. Bridgett impressed upon Bernard two things: "his father was the greatest man in all the world, and that he had to grow up just like him, the second that he was to be a priest."[322] Indeed, as a very young boy she taught him to lisp "a bishop"[323] when asked what he would be.

It seems his first experience of the juvenate was with his nurse, who: "went so far as to buy him a tiny ring which he would solemnly present to be kissed, and taught him how to give his blessing!"[324] His older brother John died as a young boy and when little Bernard was brought in to see him, he gazed at his brother for a long while before whispering in his sister's ear: "When John is dead I shall be Papa's eldest son, shan't I?"[325] The weight of the world seemed to descend on his shoulders at that moment. He was a quiet, serious boy and did not enjoy conflict. Indeed, when arguments would break out he would have no part in it until the group was reconciled and the games could resume, an interesting temperament for one who would be flung into the heat of battle later in his life. The children often played 'the Mass' in the nursery and it was quickly decided that Bernard gave the best sermons: "I can still distinctly see the quaint little figure standing in his improvised pulpit. This generally consisted of a chest of drawers, on which a towel-rail was placed and at first, he always had to stand upon a stool that his head might be visible to the congregation."[326] Bernard began school early on account of his active mind, he was only five. At school, the Masters were astonished by his gift for understanding and preaching the scriptures and remarked this to his father. At the age of eight, Bernard was sent to the Jesuit College and, although still very young, the Masters were very impressed with him and began preparing him to make his first Holy Communion. However, a dispute arose between the Jesuits and the Parish Priest, both of whom wanted the event to happen in their churches. The result was that it was postponed for some months, which Bernard found very hard: "I don't see how the place can matter a bit. It is the making that matters."[327] It would seem the Jesuits won the day and Bernard made his first Holy Communion. Dr. Kavanagh taught the children to value honesty and proper conduct. One night a visiting priest debated hotly with poor Bernard, who rarely lost his temper, and although this was sport for the priest who was amazed at the intellect of his interlocutor, Dr. Kavanagh was not pleased. Bernard was sent to bed at the appropriate hour but the next morning was marched straight to the priest's house to apologise. The priest, who was the Vicar-General for the diocese in England where Bernard's sisters where at school, was thoroughly amiable and tried to pacify the boy. Bernard stood his ground and apologised in such a way that the priest later reported: "how delighted he had been with Bernard's straightforward and manly way of acting, and was more impressed by him than ever."[328] The two men would meet later when Bernard was a young Redemptorist Cleric training for Ordination. The Vicar-General visited the Redemptorist community at Teignmouth and the two laughed about the incident and made friends over the reminiscence. However, Bernard's sister was so over ought by what she perceived as the unfairly harsh treatment of her brother that she accosted her father, who sat her down to explain: "He said that gentleman could never be too courteous to his opponent, and should always keep cool in an argument...He added that it was all the more necessary in this case, as the boy promised to be very clever and would consequently be likely to get the best of any argument he took part in."[329] A valuable lesson for all of us in humility and gentleness. Bernard was ready to be sent to college when he began to suffer with Asthma and had to employ a medicinal cigarette to find comfort during long nights of illness. His ever-faithful nurse would come often to see if she could help by lighting a fire for him and so on. He was always grateful for the love, care and affection he received in his sickness. Following the death of his father, his mother became ill and a certain misunderstanding occurred, which resulted in Bridget being sent away. Bernard was devastated and fought hard for her to stay. He maintained she was badly dealt with and Bridget entered an unhappy marriage, which only made him feel more wretched. In secret, he visited her as often as he could in the west of Ireland. Bridgett would fall upon him when he arrived and weep, calling him her "darling boy, her precious lamb"[330] and he would simply be there for her. When asked how he could put up with such a show he answered: "After my own mother, there is no woman on earth that I owe so much to; and I should be an ungrateful wretch if I didn't recognise the fact. Besides I really love her, dear old Bridgett."[331]

He attributes the early development of his vocation to his parents: "The sound, practical spirit of religion that directed every thought and action of my good parents."[332] His father, who was a doctor of some reputation, was a member of the Society of St. Vincent de Paul and attended to his: "religious duties with the greatest exactness and punctuality."[333] He attended communion, went on retreat each year and would often attend the devotions at Mt St. Alphonsus. He was a man of integrity and strong Christian convictions and would visit the poor during the winter and when he arrived home would gather his family around the fire and tell them of the: "miseries of the poor in whose cabins he had been that day, and remind us to thank God for all the favours and blessings He had bestowed on us."[334] Dr. Kavanagh gave witness to the truth by example and seems to have been a man of immense humility. Indeed, Fr. Kavanagh tells us that it was only following his death that his mother learned of the true extent of her husband's charity: "My mother heard with great surprise of many an act of charity he had performed in secret."[335] He was obviously a man who knew his scripture: "If you give something to the poor, do not let your left hand know what your right hand is doing." (Mt 6:3) He dealt quietly and gently with those less fortunate than himself and in doing so allowed those to whom he gave succour to keep their dignity. Fr. Kavanagh's mother was a woman of intense prayer: "She seemed to have no other object in life than to bring up her children in the holy love and fear of God, and in discharging that duty to sanctify her own soul."[336] This was a hardworking, Christian family: "She spent a great part of her time in prayer but used to say that duty comes first, prayer second."[337] From his earliest days, Fr. Kavanagh was brought up to value his duty. Today we often place more emphasis on our own 'rights' and entitlements but this was a family raised to value service to others.

At the age of five he began to attend the Christian Brothers School in Limerick: the Christian Brothers had opened the school in order to provide an education for the children of the poor of Limerick, which was sorely needed at the time. Fr. Kavanagh speaks very fondly of his time at the school and in particular of Rev. Mr. Kenny who taught him and who: "soon became one of the sincerest friends I ever had."[338] Although there seems to have been no incident that further fuelled his feelings of vocation to the sacred priesthood it seems likely that his exposure to great Religious and Lay examples of the Christian life helped the seed to grow slowly and steadily in his heart: "the idea of becoming a priest seems to me to have been engrafted in my mind from the very dawn of reason."[339] Although there was a strong pull to follow his father into the medical profession Bernard knew what he would become. Young Bernard enjoyed talking with the various people who came to see his father and when they asked if he would become a doctor too he would say "no" and if he felt that he could trust the discretion of the other he would say "I will be a priest."[340]

At the age of nine Bernard entered Sacred Heart College, which was run by the Jesuits. Bernard was very fond of the Jesuits and found every excuse to visit them outside of school hours, whether to serve at Mass or to ask a question of one of the Fathers. It comes as no surprise then that Bernard first thought of becoming a Jesuit. He did not know many other religious very well and although he had met Fr. Edward O'Donnell C.Ss.R. and Fr. McLaughlin C.Ss.R. he says: "as to the other Fathers at Mt. St. Alphonsus I did not even know their appearance."[341] When he was thirteen his older sister, who was by now a professed nun in Belgium, wrote to him to encourage her brother to consider his vocation.

Bernard now began to take his feelings of vocation to the Priest-hood in the Society of Jesus seriously. In the same breath, he tells us that he had no love of the Society although he had a great affection for its members who had been so kind to him: "I think that my wish to join it arose more from natural motives than supernatural."[342] Bernard began to accompany his father when he attended the retreats given to the Lay Society of St. Vincent de Paul, which were given alternately by the Jesuits and the Redemptorists and here he began to engage with the faith on an-other level: "They caused me to think seriously on eternity and enabled me to despise the passing pleasures of the hour."[343] He found the sermons of the Redemptorist Fathers stirring and in-spirational but the thought of entering the Congregation rather than the Jesuits never crossed his mind.

His father passed away in October 1879. He had suffered with heart disease for some considerable time and eventually con-tracted a cold that he found difficult to shake off. One night he was called out to the house of a poor gentleman who needed his help. Bernard's sister begged him not to go as he was too ill but he replied: "If the call were from a rich man, I certainly would not go, for I feel far too ill and the rich can always find plenty of people at their service. But I have never yet turned a deaf ear to the voice of the poor, and it is too late to begin now."[344] Pneumonia quickly set in and he passed away only three days later:

"His death was a most saintly one and his confessor, one of the Jesuits, who attended him said afterwards that he himself derived as much profit from witnessing that calm death as he would have done from a retreat."[345]

Bernard took the news that his father would not recover very hard and was inconsolable for days. However, following his father's passing, he took great comfort in his example of dying peacefully, full of faith and trust in God. Bernard visited the Jesuit community to beg their prayers for his father but they were already aware of the situation and assured him of their constancy in prayer. One lay brother, a particular favourite of Bernard, encouraged him to make a vow that if his father were to survive his illness then Bernard would enter the Society of Jesus:

"I made no vow of any kind but I prayed hard that God might in his mercy restore my father's life and asked for light for myself that I might know God's holy will and knowing, that I might do it."[346]

On his death bed, Dr. Kavanagh was consoled by the knowledge that his son intended to enter the Society of Jesus. Slowly the family got back to some state of normality although that gap left by a parent gone too soon is never fully filled. Bernard was busy with his examinations but his poor mother missed her husband terribly: "The spirits of all revived somewhat, except my poor mother's."[347] His mother became ill and Bernard became the man of the house. He took care of her and the younger children and also took over the various legal matters that followed his father's death and was more than equal to the task. That summer of 1880 his visited the shrine at Knock with his mother and: "returned with renewed fervour but without any increase of my vocation to enter the Society."[348] During the winter of 1880/81 Bernard focussed on the question of his vocation to the priesthood again and emerged in the spring a new man with the conviction that he was to offer his life as a religious.

Having discerned that his vocation did not lie with the Jesuits Bernard now began to ask God where he might offer himself. All the while he made plans to go to University and began to be excited by the idea. About that time, he made the acquaintance of a young Redemptorist, Reverend Fr. Dowling C.Ss.R. He would walk with Fr. Dowling and although they soon became friends Bernard never mentioned that he felt he had a vocation. Fr. McDonald C.Ss.R. was elected Provincial Superior and Fr. Dowling, who realised that Bernard had a vocation, arranged for the two to meet. Bernard did not know what to expect from the meeting but made his way to the Monastery. His sister later recalled that: "One short half-hour decided his future, and showed him quite plainly that God called him to be a son of St. Alphonsus. Bernard was invited to enter the congregation immediately but felt that he had not yet finished his education. The Provincial responded: "Throw it up, my boy.

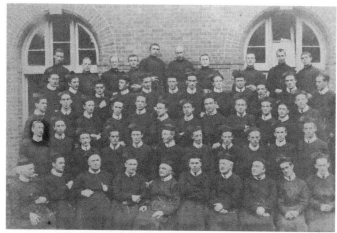

We do not need learned men so much as apostolic ones, and in God's name, I promise you, that if you make him this sacrifice, your Apostleship will be a fruitful one."[349] Bernard hesitated no longer but responded with his characteristic generosity. His mother was delighted and knew that his vocation came from God. She did however insist that he took a holiday before he entered. He needed a break after studying so hard for his exams. Bernarda and one of his sisters travelled up the Rhine and travelled through Germany, Switzerland and the Netherlands. According to his sister, he entered the Redemptorists in the London Province in order to avoid the distractions of the political situation in Ireland at the time: "he feared to be drawn into political disputes, which would, to say the least of it be sources of distraction and mental agitation, and might lesson in intensity his spiritual aims."[350] His younger brother Michael later entered Ushaw seminary in the North East of England for the same reasons. Brother Bernard entered the Redemptorist Novitiate at Bishop Eton, Liverpool, on 8th December 1882. His sister was in St. Anne's Convent nearby and wrote to invite him to visit the convent before she returned to Clapham. The response was so severe that her Mother Superior was loathe to give it to her, however Sister Kavanagh burst into fits of laughter upon reading the letter. Mother, who obviously thought the good sister had finally cracked asked how she could take it in such good humour. Sister Kavanagh replied that it was clear that Bernard had not written the letter. Not to be foiled, the sisters hatched a plan! They set out to make a pilgrimage to Bishop Eton to the Blessed Sacrament but such a heavy fog descended that it was virtually impossible to see one another. Indeed, several times they lost their way. At one point the sisters became aware of men's footsteps coming towards them but saw only "the faintest of shadows"[351] as they passed. After making a visit to the Blessed Sacrament one sister took Sr. Kavanagh and rousing the Porter asked to see Br. Kavanagh. The Porter explained that the Novices had gone to visit the Convent of St. Anne's and where not at home. The faintest of shadows had separated one from the other.

Bishop Eton Monastery

His novitiate over he made first vows in 1883 and proceeded to Clapham to visit his sister at last and they spent many cherished hours together laughing about the infamous letter. From there Bernard travelled to the House of Studies in Teignmouth. Rev. Fr. Bridgett C.Ss.R., who achieved eminence as a writer, had known Bernard's father while he served as Rector in the Redemptorist community at Limerick and held him in high esteem. Fr. Bridgett visited Teignmouth often and was in a position to visit both Bernard and his sister in Clapham as her confessor and so the two kept in touch. Bernard admired "this truly great man"[352] and felt privileged to have known him and it certainly seems that the admiration was mutual. Indeed, Fr. Bridgett wrote to Fr. Kavanagh while the latter was serving in the Parish of St. Josephs in Kilmarnock, Scotland, a letter discussing Our Lady and the development of the devotion to her.

Fr. Bridgett continues the letter with the news that a new organ has been placed by the front door to the church in Clapham, which is now situated to the right of the sanctuary, and encourages Fr. Kavanagh telling him how the community flourished at the time. This great man must have had a deal of affection for Fr. Kavanagh to be writing such letters to him. He signs off: "All would send you a hearty Christmas greeting if they knew I was writing, your devoted servant, Fr. T. Bridgett C.Ss.R."[353] While at Teign-

mouth Bernard's health began to deteriorate and he was sent home to see if he would benefit from "his native air"[354]. While there he spent time to visit his mother, who was an invalid. Indeed, the Redemptorists took every opportunity to send him to visit his poor mother when he was in Ireland. Families have ever been important to the Congregation and still today we are encouraged to see our families often and show the families of confrères every courtesy when they come to visit. Upon returning home for the second time since he had departed to follow his vocation Bernard found that his younger brother Michael had begun considering his own calling in life and Bernard was able to influence his mother so that he was sent to Austria to the Jesuit College at Feldkirch in the Austrian Alps.

While there Michael became convinced that his vocation was to the Priesthood and determined, with Bernard's advice, to study at Ushaw College in the North East of England and began his studies in 1889. Bernard served as Clark of Works in the community at Teignmouth during the construction of a new wing, but this was probably more of an effort to keep him out in the fresh air than anything else. Being a keen student, he felt much aggrieved at the loss of time to study his books but this was something he would have to get used to as God had purpose for him outside of the life of an academic.

Convent of Notre Dame, Teignmouth

He remained at Teignmouth until 1890, when in December he was sent to Clapham to prepare for his Ordination to the Sacred Priesthood. He was ordained on 20th Dec 1890 in St. George's Cathedral, Southwark, by Bishop John Baptist Butt of Southwark, who was bishop between 1885 and 1897, when he resigned. His ordination seemed to affect Fr. Kavanagh and his sister, now in a convent in Antwerp, explains that he took on a new character: "He at once assumed the role of the elder, and I gladly yielded it to him, only too glad to have so strong a staff to lean upon."[355] As the years passed he seemed to grow into his Priesthood and we are told: "Increasing years only added depth and breadth to his sympathetic loving heart."[356] His relationship with his sister grew to a more spiritual level and he became her one true friend and counsellor. Though they were often apart for a long time, eleven years passed between their first and second meetings, they were bonded by more than blood. They were a strength and grace for one another, when life was hard. They had always been close but their religious bond elevated their relationship to the service of God: "You know, Kathleen, both you and I will have a very great reward in the next life, because we have not only given up all things to follow Our Lord, but we have given up each other and that is something much more!"[357] In 1899, Bernard's mother, who had been an invalid for nearly 24 years, was on her death bed. The family gathered to her bed side and the Redemptorists arranged some mission work for Fr. Bernard near-by so that he could remain with his mother. However, she passed away quite suddenly on the 20th June and Fr. Bernard, who was giving a mission at the time returned home as soon as he could. He buried his mother with the care only a son could offer and was a consoling influence for his grieving family. During the next year his sister's health deteriorated rapidly and she called upon him to visit her. He came as soon as he was able in August of that year and listened patiently to her circumstances. Never an impulsive man, he discerned that he would pray upon her situation for the next three days and say Mass for her intention hoping that God would tell him what he should advise her to do, but he made his sister promise to abide by God's command. Three days later he came to her and told her that she was being tested by God and must persevere, a virtue much prized by Redemptorists! Eventually this advice was found to be good advice and her situation improved but Fr. Kavanagh had worked very hard behind the scenes to secure an improvement in her circumstances without ever telling her.

Fr. Kavanagh carried his characteristically quiet nature, humility and charity into his Redemptorist life and spent the 24 years following his ordination as a missioner and travelled the length and breadth of the land bringing the good news of plentiful redemption to the poor and most abandoned: "in this capacity he travelled, giving missions at various times to nearly all the industrial centres of Great Britain."[358] Redemptorists are told to preach by simplicity of life and language: we preach to all not to an intellectual elite. Venerable Joseph Passerat C.Ss.R. said: "A badly written sermon has no more chance of piercing the heart than a rusty and crooked nail has of entering a wall."[359]

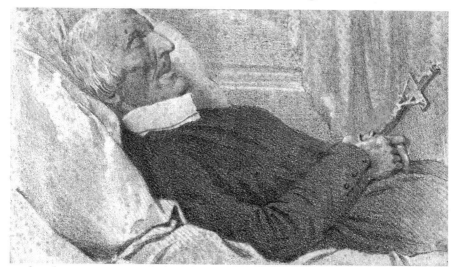

Indeed, Fr. Kavanagh spoke well as his obituary in the tablet recalls: "He was a gifted speaker, and his facile eloquence never failed to arrest attention and move the hearts of his hearers."[360] Just as with his sister in the parlour of her convent, he had a simple way of speaking which set the listener at ease and opened their hearts to the still small voice of calm.

In 1914, upon the outbreak of war at the age of 50, Fr. Bernard was missioned to be a forces chaplain and rose to this new challenge with his usual generosity. His commission to the Royal Army Chaplains Department is dated 27th September 1914 and the Chronicles of St. Mary's Clapham notes the following on

18th November 1914· "Fr Kavanagh (Captain) Chaplain to HM Forces pays us a visit."[361] He was in fact the base chaplain at Purfleet Barracks in Essex, which was a Gunpowder Magazine and anti-aircraft station during the First World War. In March 1916, a German Zeppelin was brought down by the anti-aircraft gun and the garrison received a special prize from the Mayor of London. Through the early months of the war Fr. Kavanagh remained at Purfleet and was able to make regular visits to Clapham. However, on 4th December 1914, Fr. Kavanagh was sent to the front and he was replaced by Fr. Thomas Bradley C.Ss.R., who went on to join the Royal Navy and served at Jutland. Fr. Kavanagh went to Egypt with his regiment the West Kent Regiment to join the Egyptian Expeditionary Force as the British Army pushed towards Gaza and on to Jerusalem. In May 1915, Fr. Kavanagh visited the community in Bishop Eton, Liverpool: "Fr. Kavanagh has many interesting stories to tell of life in camp and of the Army."[362] On 30th August 1915, Fr. Kavanagh made his way home from the front to visit Clapham and remained for dinner, no doubt a welcome break, but also a great privilege to be able to leave the front: our Catholic chaplains accompanied the men into the most fearful situations and were famed for their bravery winning a number of medals and so one can well understand the need for a trip home to the familiar. His final visit of 1915 came on the 5th October according to the Chronicles. 1916 was a critical year in the First World War: the battles of the Somme, on land, and Jutland, upon the waves, helped to turn the tide of the war. The Chronicles do not mention whether he returned home during 1916 but I can only assume with the fighting reaching its apex he was kept very busy and if he managed to return at all it was probably very brief. On 23rd March 1917 Fr. Kavanagh was with his regiment the 2/4 Royal West Kents E.E.F. and wrote to his sister. She was obviously unhappy at him putting himself in harm's way, as any sister would have been, but he soon reminded her of his duty: "Your warlike letter set me off in a fit. Why should everybody else be encouraged to do their bit while your family are wrapped up in cotton wool? I am thriving and in excellent health in spite of rain and sand holes at night and scorching days."[363] For security reasons, he was not able to divulge either the location of the expeditionary force nor its objectives, however he did his best to give a taste of daily life at the front: "Yesterday the Desert Column made a further march into Palestine amid miles of barley and downs clad in beautiful wild flowers. I rode beside the Band of our Battalion which was loudly playing popular music to hearten the heavily laden men. Not like the Israelites of old, nor like the medieval crusaders but in his own stolid unimaginative way T. Atkins took possession of the land of promise to the strains of "Men of Harlech" or the "Girl I left behind me" …Everywhere we stop we set to work to dig trenches, train our guns, place outposts and make every preparation for an attack."[364]

On the 24th December 1917 Very Rev. Fr. Provincial, Fr. John Charlton C.Ss.R. received a letter from one R.J. Pendell 2/4 The Queen's Brigade E.E.F., the only Catholic officer in the battalion, informing him of that Fr. Kavanagh had been killed in action: "He was hit in the head by a Turkish bullet and remained unconscious until he died a few hours later. I was within a few yards of Father Kavanagh when he was hit, he had come quite up to the front line, and was praying at the time with a wounded man."[365] Fr. Kavanaghs sister in the Convent, was notified by Fr. Charlton by telegram sent from Bishop Eton, which read: "Superior Notre Dame Convent LPOOL Fr Kavanagh died of wounds 21st Dec please inform Sister."[366] Fr. Kavanagh was cared for in his ministry by his batman, servant, 200962 Private T.F. Hitchens of the 2/4 The Queen's Regt. 5th Batt E.E.F. who remained with him to the end. On 12th March 1918, Private Hitchens wrote to Fr. Kavanagh's sister from Palestine to tell her of his affection for her brother. He had been assigned to Fr. Kavanagh when he joined the regiment in February 1917: "and was with him all the time, and got very attached to him, as he was so good and kind to all, a fine priest whom all respected, Catholic and non-Catholic alike."[367] Private Hitchens became a Catholic and with the help of Fr. Kavanagh learnt to serve at Mass, something we often take for granted and yet something Hitchens felt was very special, he says: "I had the honour of serving his last Mass in Jerusalem, at the Convent of Perpetual Adoration."[368] Private Hitchens told Sister Kavanagh not only about the duties her brother carried out but also about his character: "Every Sunday he preached a sermon, and his words always seemed to fit in, help, and make us try again. On the march, he wouldn't ride his horse very often, he would say, to walk with the boys made him remember how 'Our Lord and Blessed Lady trod the same ground'. I know of one day he marched with us 17 miles, happy, explaining to us all about the places we were going through. His life was all sacrifice, to the end, and he died with the boy he was tending in his arms."[369]

This letter only reached its destination on 21st May after having on board a mail ship that had been sunk: the original letter is written in purple pencil which has run down the page. The letter lay on the bottom for some months before the correspondence was recovered. In fact, Fr. Kavanagh had been called forward from the advanced dressing station to tend to the poor wounded man. A letter from a Captain of the Royal Artillery, whose name is unknown reports: "He heard that some poor fellow was asking for a priest, and he went forward to him in full view of the enemy, and eye-witnesses say that he appeared to speak to the man, and then to pray, and he had just made the sign of the cross when a bullet hit him in the head. They got him away to the field ambulance in Jerusalem but he never recovered consciousness and died that night in Jerusalem."[370] An extract from a letter of Staff-Captain Bernard J. Smith, then serving in Palestine, gives a less gentle account of Fr. Bernard's passing: "We had a little scrap yesterday in which we were successful. Such a scrap is not worthwhile for the papers to mention now a days, but in the Boer War it would have filled the front page of the Daily Mail. One of our RC Padres, a Father Kavanagh, was killed. He was actually pronouncing absolution over a man and was just saying 'Amen' when he stopped one with his head and never recovered consciousness. He died during the night. It was his Mass I attended last

Sunday. He was a good man. RC Padres are thought well of out here. People cannot understand why they go into the front line. A splendid death wasn't it?"[371] He was buried in the German Hospice Military Cemetery, Mount of Olives, Jerusalem, Palestine. However, a letter received in Feb 1921 from the Imperial War Graves Commission, notes that: "Owing to the necessity of collecting scattered graves for the sake of future preservation, and the removal of certain cemeteries, which were situated in places unsuitable for permanent retention, it has been found necessary to exhume the bodies buried in certain areas."[372] The letter continues, noting: "The body of Captain The Reverend B. Kavanagh, A.C.D. has therefore been removed from the German Hospice Military Cemetery and re-buried in Jerusalem Military Cemetery, Palestine."[373] Fr. Bernard's belongings were sent home to Clapham.

Many of his personal items were then forwarded on to his sister. One Sargent of the Royal Army Medical Core, who knew Fr. Kavanagh from his many visits to the field hospital wrote to express his affection for the 'Pilgrim Priest'.

It is often the case that military chaplains have a good working relationship with the medical branch as is evidenced here: "Fr. Kavanagh came over to him [a dying man], he was in awful pain poor lad, and the Fr. prayed over him and gave him his blessing, after he had passed away, I wrote to his mother and told her all I could and I mentioned this although he was not a Catholic, and it gave her great consolation. He came down twice since he went from us, and each time came to see me, the last time I saw him, he was looking well, and still very happy."[374] Chaplain Donnell C.F. wrote of Fr. Bernard describing his "unflinching courage and self-sacrifice" and continues, saying: "There are many things in the lives of such men – and more particularly in the lives of priests – which are not visible to the public eye but which are an influence for good upon all who come into contact with them...Your brother's name will be revered and the men, Catholic and Protestant alike, for and amongst whom he laboured. This is no small matter in these days, when heroism is so common."[375] We may wonder what the other officers felt regarding chaplains and in Fr. Kavanagh's case we have the answer from Chaplain Donnell: "The work of a priest is different from his brother officers; they scarcely know what it is, and yet they are the first to appreciate him for his devotion to it."[376] Chaplain Donnell offers an insight into the dynamic role of the Chaplain to the Forces: "I believe that God is making use of the devoted labour of his priests in the army, not only for the immediate purposes of saving the souls of the dying, but also for breaking down prejudice..."[377] If you were to visit a military chaplaincy today this is what you would find, men and women of different denominations working together to the glory of God. It had been Fr. Bernard's ambition to die in the Holy Land and his fellow chaplains believed he would have been pleased: "It is fitting that such a great Redemptorist should lay down his life, in the land so near the spot of our Redemption."[378] Indeed, one chaplain says: "He is, I am sure, a saint in heaven, and I beg of you to ask him to pray for us who are left to carry on the work, that our lives and efforts may be as blessed and fruitful as were his."[379] There are so many letters from the front from those who wished to convey their sympathies to the family of Fr. Kavanagh that it would be difficult to discuss them all here but it really is a testimony to the affect he had on those he met. One Sargent Major wrote from 24th Stationary Hospital E.E.F. on 11th March 1918. He said of Fr. Kavanagh that: "at all times he had a cheering word for any of us, especially to those whose duty it was to control the destinies of others. I am profoundly certain he looked upon the non-commissioned rank of the army in the same light as he himself did to those who professed his faith, and that we all of us were morally and spiritually guiding those of our unit, and therefore bound together in a sacred cause."[380] Indeed, on the occasion that Fr. Bernard became ill or was wounded and was sent to the hospital train for treatment and rest he was always pleased to see the Sargent Major: "His remark on my greeting him was 'Well Sargent Major you see I am come home.' That is how we have always felt when officers and others have left the unit that we were a big family and the loss was felt. When he got back to us it gave one a glimpse of our expected pleasure on our return home."[381] When Fr. Kavanagh's death was announced in the Redemptorist parish of St. Edmund's in Edmonton, London, copies of his last letter home were published for each house in the parish and a fund was raised to erect a stained-glass window in his memory. In the end, £250 was raised and the window was unveiled in May 1918 and depicted the crucifixion with St. Edmund and St. George on either side. A parishioner, Mr. Frank Hanley, had kept his families copy and sent it to the Redemptorist archives for posterity. It was obviously a source of inspiration to him as he later wrote an article for the parish newsletter about it. Having read the letter, it seems a shame to dissect it here but rather more appropriate to give a new generation of readers a chance to listen to the voice of a Redemptorist priest at the front speaking to us one hundred years since. Father Kavanagh was a man of faith, free for God and free to serve his people. He cared deeply about communicating the faith especially to the poor and most abandoned and to that end he accepted a mission to the most dangerous places on Earth to be with those who needed the face of mercy in their world. The passion of those who wrote to speak well of him is truly astonishing and shows his influence and yet, like his father before him, he was a quiet unassuming man who did his duty to God and who sought God in his fellow Man. I feel the best way to end his account is with these words: "I can assure you that his devotion is best symbolized by 'Greater love hath no man, than he lay down his life for his friend.' By going out to a mortally wounded man he carried his life in his hands and the rewards which he doubtless covets is his. 'In as much as ye did to the least of these...' His life will remain as a living example of a life well spent and of one who acquitted himself like a man."[382]

Our Mother of Perpetual Succour.

Pray for him.

St. Alphonsus and all our Redemptorist saints.

Pray for us.

REV. FR. OLIVER CONROY C.SS.R. R.A.F.

Born   1907

Professed 1927

Ordained 1932

Died   1985

Fr. Oliver was born in "St. Bede's own beloved town"[383] of Jarrow, Tyneside in 1907. His sole desire was that he would grow up to become a priest and his mother, Ellen, and father, William, did everything they could to encourage him in this desire. Indeed, it seems to have been taken for granted that this would be his vocation in life by his whole family. On the outbreak of war two of Oliver's family went to serve their country and were soon followed by those who came of age during the war. It was a difficult and uncertain time for families all over the country and the Conroy family was no different. Oliver's sister, Grace, had taken a great interest in his vocation and felt called to the religious life, but the separation of war made her long to be with her family. However, in 1916, with the Battle of the Somme under-

Way Grace entered the Convent of Mercy in Sunderland. This was a big decision, it would have meant being largely cut off from news of her family and must have been very unsettling. Still, a religious sister once told me that if God has given us a vocation to serve him, he gives us the grace to be able to fulfil it, all we have to do is say "YES"! In 1919 with the war over and the process of rebuilding Europe underway, Oliver was waiting to enter the seminary at Ushaw College. He had discerned that his vocation was to the missionary life: "For some years now I had felt drawn to that higher state of life as a development of my vocation to priesthood."[384] While the Congregation is a Preaching order and not strictly a missionary order it has always been within the mission given by Alphonsus to go to the margins of society to those who are poor and most abandoned. While he was waiting to enter his sister learned of "a little college"[385] in Liverpool, which was for applicants to the Congregation of the Most Holy Redeemer: "It seemed that a nun, who had just had a brother ordained in the Congregation, knowing from my sister of my desires, had immediately recommended the Juvenate as the place I was seeking."[386] Oliver set off to visit this sister who had suggested the Congregation to him and from there was sent to visit the Rector of St. Bennet's, the local Redemptorist community but was told he was told he was too young, he was still only thirteen years old. Still, the meeting had gone well and Fr. Rector had been suitably impressed by Oliver and so had made communications to the Juvenate at Bishop Eton, Liverpool, that he should be put on the waiting list to enter.

All he could do now was wait patiently and pray that if this was God's desire for him, that he would help it come to pass. It was at this time that he took his younger brother, Gilbert, back to the school of the Sisters of Mercy. Mother superior, again suitably impressed by this young man and his desires to leave all and follow Christ, offered him a deal: he would come a couple of days a week to school there and she would obtain for him entry into the Juvenate as soon as possible. On 25th January 1921 Oliver left home to begin his journey of vocation at the Juvenate of the Congregation of the Most Holy Redeemer in Bishop Eton, Liverpool. While there he endeavoured to become more and more familiar with the history and mission of the Congregation and felt his zeal for the life grow. This time of first encountering the charism of the Congregation felt like coming home. Indeed, a genuine experience of happiness. One is reminded of the men on the road to Emmaus: "Did our hearts not burn within us as he spoke..." (Lk 21:32) On the 8th July 1926 Oliver was deemed fit to enter the Noviciate at the Redemptorist house of Kinnoul in Perth, Scotland. Upon entering the Noviciate, Fr. Conroy, then Br. Conroy, wrote these words: "As Novice, then, in the Sacred Heart of Jesus, I place the trust of my Holy Perseverance, even as I have always done, the trust of my Holy Vocation."[387] At the conclusion of the Noviciate year on 15th August 1927 Oliver made his first vows as a Redemptorist and three years later on the 7th September 1930 was finally professed in the Congregation of the Most Holy Redeemer. In September 1932 Oliver was ordained to the Sacred Priesthood and began working on the mission staff in Perth. This was deemed to be the dream appointment as the main concern of the Congregation was to preach missions. He moved to Clapham and worked in the Parish. In 1939 upon the outbreak of the Second World War the Redemptorists offered men to serve as chaplains to the armed forces and in 1941 he was commissioned as a chaplain to the Royal Air Force. The Royal Flying Corps had been formed in 1912 and by 1914 the Royal Navy had its own branch, which eventually became the Fleet Air Arm. However, the R.A.F. as it exists today was not formed until the 1st April 1918. In 1919, Padre Viener, a former RN chaplain helped to form the R.A.F. Chaplains Branch, whose motto is: "to serve not to be served."[388] During the Second World War around 1000 chaplains passed into the Branch and served across the front line and in Air Stations. R.A.F. Chaplains, like their counterparts in the Army, carry rank. Their day to day routine began and ended with the Divine Office after which they would have time to deal with any correspondence before visiting the sick or those in prison. After lunch, a chance to walk the base and visit the aircrew either as they moved about the base or in their workshops. Next the chaplains were able to visit those living in married quarters and a chance to check in with the Commanding Officer before returning to the office to be available for any persons who wished to visit them. Fr. Conroy was appointed to the 2nd Tactical Air Force, formed on 1st June 1943 at RAF Bracknell, which is presumably where Fr. Conroy was based at that time, to further strengthen the attacking force of the RAF:

"The Command was part of the Fighter Command and controlled two operational groups (Nos 2, 83) plus No 38 Wing. On 15th November it transferred to the Allied Expeditionary Force as part of the build-up for the invasion of Europe. The bombers of No 2 Gp and the ground attack aircraft, primary Spitfires and Typhoons plus the ubiquitous Auster, of No 83 Gp and, when formed, No 84 Gp, provided the on the spot fire-power that became such a decisive feature of the Allied progress through France and into Germany following the invasion of June 1944. The squadrons undertook a wide range of tasks, building up and impressive score of enemy aircraft, tanks, vehicles and trains. The German generals were convinced that the stranglehold wielded by such tactical air power was decisive in the last 12 months of war. With the conflict in Europe over and the RAF maintaining a presence in Germany it was decided to rename the Command; on 15th July 1945 the 2nd TAF disbanded to be replaced by the British Air Forces of Occupation."[389]

In 1944, Fr. Oliver landed on 'Juno' beach, Normandy, with the 2nd Tactical Air Force as part of the invasion force. After the war he left the R.A.F. and returned to the Redemptorist community at Bishop Stortford, where he became Rector for two terms. He then moved on to spend six years with the Redemptorist Travelling Missions in Wales. In 1964 Fr. Conroy was sent to Southern Rhodesia, now Zimbabwe, where he helped in the training of new Redemptorists from the local area. He also worked in this capacity in South Africa where in 1980 his brother Gilbert was murdered after offering a hitch hiker a lift close to their mission centre at Modimong in the Rustenburg area. The loss of his brother in such tragic circumstances hurt Oliver deeply. In 1983 Fr. Oliver retired to Heathfield in Cape Town. He had become very frail by this point in his life and following surgery he passed away on the 27th May 1985.

Our Mother of Perpetual Succour.

Pray for him.

St. Alphonsus and all our Redemptorist saints.

Pray for us.

REV. FR. EDWARD JOHN GIBSON C.SS.R. C.F.

Born 1911

Professed 1933

Ordained 1935

Died 1982

Edward was born on 11th November 1911 at Southall, near London. His mother and father were originally from the North of England. His father, Francis, was from Carlisle and his mother was from Salford. He was baptised, confirmed and received Holy Communion in his parish of St. Anselm in Southall. It seems Edward may well have been destined for the Redemptorists from the beginning and at his confirmation he took the name Alphonsus! In the absence of any Catholic Schools in the area Edward attended the local Church of England schools and received a good education until the construction of St. Anselm's School, when he was transferred across. While attending a school mission given by Fr. George Nicholson C.Ss.R. he felt called to the missionary work of the Congregation: "Although there were plenty of missionary societies, I came to the conclusion that the Redemptorists was the one, for giving missions."[390] So many vocations have been inspired by the preaching of missions and this remains a focus of the Congregation to this day. One night after choir practice in the church four of the choristers, including Edward remained behind. While walking down the nave of the church to the door Edward felt a strange desire to turn around and look at the sanctuary.

All the lights in the church were off and yet his gaze was drawn to one of the windows. The other boys turned to see what he was looking at, and this is what they saw: "On one of the stained glass window panes, a figure of Our Crucified Saviour gradually appeared. It seemed to come out of nowhere. We all stood awe stricken to the spot, no one had as it were the strength to kneel down and pray, because we were so overcome by a kind of fear. It stayed for about 2 minutes and went away. When I got home, my mother wanted to know why I was so pale, and so I related it to her."[391] His mother, naturally, assumed it had been an optical illusion but Edward maintained that, as the four of them had seen it together, it could not be. Undeterred he told Fr. Buckle, the Parish Priest of St. Anselm's, who said it could have been a vision and told Edward that something would come of it. Edward prayed for the vocation to preach Christ Crucified in the Congregation and after attending Campion House Osterley for several years, where his vocation was fostered and encouraged, he was accepted to enter the Redemptorist Novitiate at Kinnoul and entered on 13th July 1929.

Brother Edward was clothed in the Holy Habit of the Congregation on 14th August 1929 and made his first vows on 15th August 1930 at which time he was sent to Hawkstone Hall, in Shropshire, to study for the Priesthood.

Edward struggled with his studies, however when few believed him capable he was supported by Fr. Leo Kirk C.Ss.R. who wrote to Fr. Provincial to recommend that he had the requisite talent necessary to continue his studies and to make final vows. Fr. Leo highlighted that not everyone had the same strengths and Br. Gibson had in fact passed his exams. He had a rugged, simple faith which carried him through this difficult time and was a reflection of his no nonsense Cockney approach to life. His strong and positive disposition would later carry him through his trials as a chaplain during the war. He was ordained at Hawkstone Hall on the 8th September 1935 and began the work of preaching Our Crucified Lord that he had ever prayed for.

Upon the outbreak of the Second World War in 1939 he put his name forward as a volunteer to serve as a chaplain in the army. He was accepted and seemed well suited to this ministry. He was commissioned into the Royal Army Chaplains Department and sent to the front in North Africa, however he was captured and taken as a Prisoner of War. He was held in a Prisoner of War (POW) camp in Italy and remained there until the Italian surrender on the 8th September 1943. On that day the Italians abandoned the camp and he walked out of the gates and managed to hide with a Redemptorist community in Northern Italy for some time. Eventually, a suitable guide was found who promised to lead Fr. Gibson to the Swiss boarder and so to neutral territory and safety. However, this guide betrayed Fr. Gibson to the Germans and he was taken once again as a POW to Germany where he would sit out the rest of the war. He was eventually released upon the German surrender in 1945 and finally made his way home to Clapham. It is terrible to think of the hardships he must have endured while a captive and to think of the relief that must have taken hold of him as he crossed the threshold of the monastery once more and realised he was not going back to his cell. The Royal Army Chaplains Department Museum, at Amport House near Andover, houses a number of exhibits from men who were POWs, including a carved wooden paten engraved with the words "Panis Angelicus", bread of Angels and hymn books written on cigarette paper. These items were lovingly crafted and helped them men hold onto hope in their dire predicament. Fr. Edward 'Gibbo' Gibson C.Ss.R. C.F. was demobbed at Christmas 1945 and it is believed he was then appointed to Erdington Abbey.

In 1948, having spent a long time getting over his traumatic time in captivity he was posted to Bishop's Stortford and was again moved in 1953 to Sunderland. He came to Clapham to visit the community on the occasion of the Coronation of Her Majesty Queen Elizabeth II, it seems appropriate to include the following entry from the chronicles:

"2nd June 1953: Coronation Day. Despite the fact that spectators in their thousands took up their positions on the coronation route yesterday afternoon, some of the community determined not to miss the pomp, colour and pageantry of the procession. Fathers Lonergan, E. Gibson and Thomas, a member of the Canadian Province, said Mass at 2am and left for the coronation route at 3 o' clock. Later on, Fr. Thornton also joined the spectators. The rest of the community were content to watch the service and procession on a television set, which was hired for the momentous occasion. The splendour and solemnity of the historical occasion will never be forgotten by those who

witnessed it, and during the procession after the coronation ceremony in Westminster Abbey, there took place one of the greatest demonstrations of popular enthusiasm ever witnessed in London. In her broadcast to the nation, the Queen begged of Almighty God to bless all her people."[392]

He was officially moved to Clapham in 1954 to serve as the business manager for 'Novena' Magazine. He spent the following years between the community in Sunderland and Erdington Abbey. Erdington was his final appointment and he began to suffer terribly with slipped discs in his back. Fr. Brookes grandmother and her daughter came to look after him more and more as he became more immobile. He spent the final 8 years of his life virtually confined to his bed in Erdington. His room was full of his stamp collection and souvenirs from visits to the shrine at Lourdes, a place very special in his heart. One confrère notes: "His little statue of Our Lady of Lourdes, balancing precariously on the bookcase and shrouded at various times of the day in tobacco smoke, watched over him and visitors alike."[393] He had a tremendous devotion to Our Lady of Lourdes and so it seems proper that he should make his way home to the Father on Her feast day. He was laid to rest in the cemetery of the Redemptorist church at Erdington. Fr. Edward would be especially remembered for being good company, his love of debating with his confrères, always it seems with a twinkle in his eye, his great devotion to Our Lady and loyalty to the Royal Family, and for his passion for the study of heraldry. He was a kindly, honest and hardworking man who did not complain for his ill fortune in the war but who set to work once more bringing the love of God to those in need.

Our Mother of Perpetual Succour.

Pray for him.

St. Alphonsus and all our Redemptorist saints.

Pray for us.

VERY REV. FR. JOSEPH HULL C.SS.R.

Born   1863

Professed 1883

Ordained 1890

Died   1932

Father Hull was born on 19th October 1863 in Bootle near Liverpool, then part of Lanca- shire. From his earliest years young Joseph enjoyed playing at saying the Holy Mass: he would erect altars, attempt to fashion thuribles from com- mon household items and speak of his future as a priest. His parents Joseph and Eliza- beth Hull encouraged him in thinking on the things of God. In 1873, he was sent to the Jes- uit school of St. Francis Xavier's College near the Redemptorist

Parish of Bishop Eton in Liverpool. Fr. Hull described the fol- lowing year, 1874, as the "darkest and brightest"[394] of his life: it seems he had fallen into a life of vice. However, that year he was to make his first Holy Communion and it was the three day re- treat that preceded his reception of Our Blessed Lord that seems to have turned his life around. Indeed, he entered both the Sodality of Our Blessed Lady and the Confraternity of the Sa- cred Heart at college. The Confraternity recommended fort- nightly reception of Holy Communion to its members, a prac- tice which Fr. Hull followed meticulously as a young man. As might be expected young Joseph desired to enter the Society of Jesus and yet he relates that he felt no real call to it but was so very impressed by the life of its members. In 1877, Joseph's father passed away and his mother, now alone, could not afford the school fees. However, the society permitted Joseph to continue his studies free of pension. A year later in 1878, things had deteriorated: the business begun by Joseph Sr. in order to support his family had failed and young Joseph was forced to leave school to assist with the business and seek his own support. He was placed as an apprentice in the Cotton Brokers Office. Joseph disliked the work and from his first day was miserable, calling the office a 'den of Satan'. He had been plucked out of the protected environment of school life and found himself among "irreligious and immoral companions"[395]. Eventually, Joseph became used to life in the office and enjoyed spending time with his companions, whose behaviour he no longer found shocking. Yet, each visit to the public house or the theatre brought him feelings of bitterness and regret, which today we may find rather over dramatic but to Joseph this was a genuine indication that he was not in the right place. He began to visit Bishop Eton for confession and then to attend the Holy Sacrifice of the Mass. One day, while out walking with a Redemptorist Father in the gardens at Bishop Eton, which at the time were extensive, he was asked if he had ever felt called to enter the congregation. Joseph replied that he had not, but the priest pressed further asking him to pray to Our Mother of Perpetual Succour for the grace. Joseph felt this was absurd at the time and yet he did begin to pray to Our Lady for the grace to give his life over in service as a Redemptorist. Joseph had a friend who was in training for the Priesthood and who noticed that Joseph had become a changed man since he began work at the office and often tried to persuade him to re-orient his life towards God. He encouraged Joseph to read the 'Life of the Curé of Ars', at which point a curious change seems to have come over Joseph, as he described:

"I commenced it with great reluctance, but when reading one of his sermons, a ray of Divine light struck my heart. I felt God's all winning call "follow me"."[396]

From that moment he resolved to become a priest and immediately went to give thanks for the intercession of Our Mother of Perpetual Succour, whom he credited with the graces he had received that had so enabled him to hear the voice of God in his life. Joseph had been praying for a call to the Priesthood in the Congregation of the Most Holy Redeemer and he now discerned his vocation to lie with the Congregation. He asked the advice of his confessor and wrote to the Provincial, who was Very Rev. Fr. Coffin C.Ss.R., who told him that he would meet with him in the autumn to discuss a way forward. Having given himself over to the vocation God had given him, he now felt all the temptations of the World all the more keenly and had to remain strong in order that his resolve might not waver. In preparation for his entrance into the Congregation Joseph received lessons in Latin, Greek, French and English. He also broke off his apprenticeship but found his greatest difficulty lay in ensuring the security of his family. The business was not succeeding and his family was struggling, but Joseph heard the call of the Lord to have courage and to follow him and so he trusted in the providence of God to care for his family. In fact, he soon found a suitable gentleman to take over the family business and his mother was pleased. He told her of his desire to enter the congregation and she gave thanks to God for "conferring so great a favour upon the family."[397] Indeed, every barrier to his following his vocation broke down one after another and Joseph gave thanks to God:

"May God and His ever Blessed Mother, truly of Perpetual Succour, ever be praised and give to me the crowning gift of final perseverance in the Congregation."[398]

Br. Joseph entered the Novitiate at Bishop Eton in 1882 and on 1st November 1883 he made his profession of vows and was sent to the house of studies at Teignmouth. On 10th September 1890 he completed his higher studies for the Priesthood and was ordained. Soon after his ordination he was sent as a professor to the Juvenate in Limerick, where he was also appointed Socius, assistant to Fr. Director. In 1894, he was recalled to Bishop Eton, where a new Juvenate had been established and was appointed Fr. Director to the Juvenate and began educating boys in preparation for religious life as they discerned their vocation to become priests in the Congregation. His success in this post led to his appointment as Rector of Bishop Eton in 1901. He remained in this post for six years, having been re-appointed after his first term of office had ended. Later in 1907 he was nominated as Rector of St. Mary's Clapham. However, after his years of busy ministry and high responsibility Fr. General gave permission for him to move to St. Bennett's in Sunderland for "three years rest"[399]. During this time he was free from the "cares, worries and burdens of very responsible and exacting offices."[400] In fact, during this period in the North East of England, Fr. Hull was able to devote himself to the Redemptorist way of life and to the preaching of missions. These years, he described as the happiest of his life. In 1912, he was appointed to be the Provincial Superior of the English Province of the Congregation by Fr. General, who paid tribute to Fr. Hull's "self-sacrificing charity and spirit of observance."[401] Residing as Provincial in St. Mary's Clapham, Fr. Hull was often engaged in hearing confessions, visiting the sick and preaching. His genial disposition, his kind and sympathetic ways soon endeared him to the parishioners and he was very popular.

When Fr. General had written to Fr. Hull to enquire whether he felt able to accept the post of Provincial for the next Triennium, he also informed Fr. Hull of some of the upcoming developments in the Congregation that would be likely to affect him during his tenure. There was to be a foundation at Pretoria, South Africa, and he would be asking for missionaries from the English Province to go to establish this new mission. So it was that during his service as Provincial three Fathers, Fr. Thomas Creagh C.Ss.R., Fr. John Burke C.Ss.R. and Fr. Leo Kirk C.Ss.R. were sent as the founding members of the South African mission.

Their work was blessed with success and soon more men were needed to continue the good work the Lord had begun in Pretoria. It was this development that led to Fr. Hull visiting Rome, during which time he met with Pope Pius X. Upon his return to the English Province he made a visitation to all of the houses of the Congregation in the Province. At each house he preached on the impressions the Holy Father had left upon him and imparted the Papal Blessing.

On 6th August 1914, following the outbreak of the First World War Cardinal Bourne asked for the assistance of the Redemptorist Fathers in providing chaplains to the Army and the Navy.

Eventually 10 Fathers were placed at his disposal.

Two men, Frs. Charles Watson and Bernard Kavanagh C.Ss.R., made the ultimate sacrifice while serving the poor and most abandoned on the front line. Another chaplain, Fr. Thomas Bradley C.Ss.R. was the chaplain on board HMS Tiger during the Battle of Jutland. Several men were wounded and a large number were honoured for their heroic service in bringing the good news of plentiful redemption into the darkest situations. Many were decorated for their service and such decorations included the Military Cross (M.C.), the Order of the British Empire (O.B.E.) and the Distinguished Service Order (D.S.O.). Indeed, Fr. David Ahearn C.Ss.R. received the D.S.O. from the King himself at Buckingham Palace. Many of these men were trained for life in the Congregation by Fr. Hull and he surely took great pleasure in reading their names as they were often mentioned in dispatches. I am quite sure he prayed fervently that each of them would come home safe from their ministry.

In 1915, he was appointed to be Fr. Rector of Bishop Eton as well as Fr. Director of the Juvenate that he had established years before. He adored this work and felt its importance keenly but still found time to assist in the church, at Mass and in the hearing of confessions. He also preached missions, especially during

Lent. As for the Juvenate, he set about building up in the hearts of the boys the spirit of St. Alphonsus. He taught them of the devotions of St. Alphonsus to the Blessed Sacrament and the Blessed Virgin and encouraged them in devotion to Our Blessed Lady under the special title of Perpetual Succour. One brother Redemptorist said of him:

"Of him it might truthfully be said, 'Zealous Domus Dei comedit me'."[402]

The Latin translates as "for the zeal of thy house has consumed me"[403]. He spent much time in improving the church and training the choir to sing at High Mass. By his efforts, electric lighting was installed in the monastery and the church and following the cessation of hostilities at the end of the war in 1918 he erected the War Memorial, which stands outside the church at Bishop Eton today. He also installed a stained glass window depicting the Last Judgement where the old organ had stood: the organ had been dismantled and sold to make way for the new window and a new and better organ had been installed in the lower tribune, close to the altar: "...and thus the choir and the sanctuary, near and dear to his heart, were brought closer together in the church"[404]. During that same year he was appointed to St. Mary's Clapham for the third time as Minister of the House.

Besides the work of giving missions he also assisted in the work of the parish. However, in 1921, Erdington Abbey was handed over to the Redemptorists from the Benedictines who were leaving. The Redemptorists still run the parish to this day, although the abbey is no longer occupied by the Redemptorists.

Fr. Hull was a member of the first Redemptorist community at Erdington in 1921 and was again appointed to be Minister of the House. Three years later, in 1924, he was appointed to be Fr. Rector at St. Benet's in Sunderland and during his term of office he oversaw the construction of the new parochial club, which was established to bring the whole parish together to celebrate and relax together:

"To bring the people of the parish together, for their recreations, amusements, socials and gatherings, in the company of their priests in a truly Catholic atmosphere."[405]

While Rector at Sunderland he laid the foundation stone for the new infant school and oversaw the centenary celebrations in honour of St Benet at which Cardinal Bourne, who had sought his assistance over a decade earlier to provide chaplains for the forces, presided in person. In 1927, he was again appointed Fr. Provincial of what was by now the London Province of the Congregation, Ireland having formed the new Dublin Province. He once again took up residence at the Provincial house of St. Mary's, Clapham, where he set about improving the church. The size of the congregations was increasing and so the church was extended near St. Gerard's Altar.

In a similar way to the work he accomplished at Bishop Eton, the organ and choir was removed from its location over the door to the chapel of St. Alphonsus, where the organ remains to this day. The old choir gallery at the end of the church was dismantled and a new chapel to St. Alphonsus was erected near the stately spire of St. Mary's.

Some years earlier, while Rector in Sunderland, he was diagnosed with Diabetes. Fr. Hull tried not to allow this illness to take control of his life but it gradually became worse. Towards the end of his final term as provincial he suffered a severe heart attack while away giving a mission in Lincoln. He received the last sacraments but slowly recovered and was able to return to ministry in Clapham. Indeed, he remained Provincial until the end of his term of office in 1930, after which he remained in Clapham as Provincial Consultor, Spiritual Director to the Sisters of Notre Dame, Director to the Children of St. Mary's, Prefect of the Church and Confessor in the parish. Sometime later he was hearing confessions in the church at St. Mary's when he suffered a paralytic stroke and lost the use of the right side of his body. Even after this serious blow he was able to recover sufficiently to walk, with the aid of a stick, to the Oratory and the tribune where he could be present at the church services. He passed away in 1932, one of the truest servants of the Congregation: he persevered to the end as he prayed he would. He was loved by all and respected by all: a man of empathy, care and devotion. A man of devotion to the Redemptorist way of life who maintained discipline and observance of the Rule of St. Alphonsus through the example of his own authentic religious life. A man of intense prayer who had an eye trained to search the soul for those areas that needed grace and healing as well as for those areas of beauty that required cultivation. A man who rose to the challenge presented by the unprecedented events of 1914 and who ensured that those who fought on the front line were not denied the sacraments and God's healing mercy. A Redemptorist.

Our Mother of Perpetual Succour.

Pray for him.

St. Alphonsus and all our Redemptorist saints.

Pray for us.

VERY REV. FR. JOHN CHARLTON C.SS.R.

Born   1878

Professed 1897

Ordained 1901

Died   1963

Alexander Charlton was to serve as Provincial Superior during the two World Wars. He would find himself visiting the War Office and communicating with men on the front line and at sea. He would receive telegrams informing him one of his confrères had been killed and he would be the one to inform the family of the tragedy. He handled the handing over of these men's possessions after their deaths. In essence his premiership in the province went above and beyond what most Redemptorist Provincials should expect to have to deal with. Yet, this stoic man rose to the challenge supported by a deep faith and love of the Lord. If you think that is a little strong, then remember that it was his duty to send men to serve as chaplains. Some who wanted to go could not and some who were fearful of going were sent. All three chaplains who were killed in action died during his time in office and he must have felt the weight of that loss greatly. He certainly wrote to the families with tremendous sympathy and sincerity. He may well be remembered as the 'War Time Provincial' but his life amounts to more than those events. He served as Provincial Superior twice, as we have said, and he was Rector of a number of the houses of the province. He was blessed with a long life, he died at the age of 85, and during those years he observed the world change entirely. He was alive during the reign of six Supreme Pontiffs and the same number of English Monarchs!

Fr. John was born in Middlesbrough on 4th January 1878, the youngest of eight children. His father owned a colliery and had been fairly well off but at the time of John's birth the family business was in decline. Indeed, the collapse of the business soon afterwards led the family to leave Middlesbrough for South London and in a scene that reminds one of a Dickens novel John, who had not yet been baptised, left his birth place in his mother's arms. The family settled close by to the Redemptorist church of St. Mary's, Clapham. Although they were not a Catholic family, the presence of the Redemptorist fathers caught the interest of young John, whose faith deepened culminating in his reception into the church by Rev. Fr. Stevens C.Ss.R.

John spent time at prayer before the Blessed Sacrament and sought the intercession Our Mother of Perpetual Succour for the grace of receiving a vocation to serve the poor and most abandoned in the Congregation. After two years he enquired about the possibility of entered the order and was sent to the recently established Juvenate at Bishop Eton in Liverpool. There he was trained for the religious life by Fr. Joseph Hull C.Ss.R. whom he would later succeed as Provincial Superior in 1915. His conversion and the example of his life encouraged his elder sister to become a Catholic also. She later entered the Convent of Poor Clares in Arundel, where she passed away in 1900 having taken the name Sr. Mary Magdalen at her religious profession. In 1903 John received his mother into the church shortly before her death.

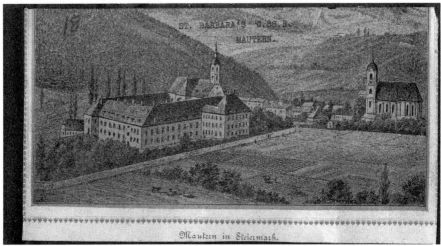

ST. BARBARA'S – C.SS.R.
MAUTERN.

Mautern in Steiermark.

After completing his novitiate he was sent to Mautern, in Austria: at the time there was no house of studies in the English Province and so the students were sent abroad. While at Mautern he encountered an elderly woman who was sick and preparing for death. She could just recall the retreat of the Imperial Forces of the Emperor Napoleon in 1812. Fr. Beverly Ahern C.Ss.R. a member of the existing Redemptorist community in Clapham remembers Fr. John speaking of this event:

"Now John Charlton was telling us this in 1949 or 1950 and he then said, which I've never forgotten. 'I wonder whether any of you will be alive in the next century to tell this story, as if you are then it means for nearly two hundred years there will be yourself, then me, then this woman in Mautern which takes you back to Napoleon in 1812. It's now April 2013 so it's just over the two hundred years spanned by three people.'"[406]

Fr. Beverly, who recently celebrated his 70th anniversary of vowed religious life is the only man in the province who was

present at Hawkstone Hall, then the house of studies, at the end of the Second World War when the London Province welcomed the students of the Cologne Province to study with them. This story will be related more fully in the afterword.

Fr. John was ordained to the Sacred Priesthood in 1901 and set about his ministry immediately, preaching missions and retreats. However, the larger part of his life was spent in office either as the Rector of one of the houses of the province or in his two spells as Provincial Superior. He was a member of the Redemptorist community at Edmonton in North London, where Fr. David Aherne C.Ss.R., chaplain to the forces with the Royal Army Chaplains Department, later served as Rector. Fr. John served as Fr. Rector at Bishop Eton and is noted in the Chronicles of St. Mary's, Clapham as arriving on 21st September 1914 to give a retreat to the brothers. He visited regularly from Bishop Eton throughout 1915 and in August news came from Fr. General that nominations for new appointments would arrive shortly on 16th August. The nominations were announced two days later than expected at Bishop Eton: Fr. John was to succeed his old teacher Fr. Hull as Provincial Superior while Fr. Hull became Rector at Bishop Eton. On 19th August 1915 the following entry was made in the chronicles:

"Fr. Charlton arrives in time for dinner and makes a speech in which he bids farewell to Fr. Hull (late prov.) and wishes hi, success endeavours and duties at Bishop Eton. The ceremony of induction of the new Provincial takes place at 3pm in the Oratory."[407]

As the war gathered pace, certain realities set in: food had to be carefully managed and the monastery made efforts to become self-sufficient by digging up large parts of the garden to grow vegetables; more and more men were needed to go to the front line and those in formation who were not yet clerics were called to the front line; and life at home was no longer safe what with the threat of invasion and zeppelin raids were now a regular occurrence. The community does not seem to have taken the zeppelin raids particularly seriously and there are even accounts of the community gathering on the roof of the monastery, which provides an excellent view across the city, to watch the zeppelins. However, in one such raid incendiary bombs were dropped killing 37 people and injuring nearly 150. Perhaps when compared to the London Blitz of the Second World War this sounds a drop in the ocean but this would have been a terrifying experience. Aircraft were still relatively new, the Royal Flying Corps was only three years old in 1915. The following week another 50 people were killed in another zeppelin raid and over 100 injured. War was no longer something fought far away or during a season. It could engulf the whole world. Yet, despite all this the life of the province had to continue and at the end of 1915 on Christmas Day Fr. Provincial celebrated the Holy Sacrifice of the Mass at the High Altar in Clapham before making visits to Bishop Stortford and Bishop Eton just before the New Year. In February 1916 Fr. John gave a mission at Barry Dock: more than ever people needed to be strong in faith and the missions helped to keep the faith alive during those dark days. On 2nd April 1916 Fr. John made his way to Sunderland to visit our parish there. The school had been badly damaged in a zeppelin raid. Fr. John was very active during these years making regular visits to all the houses. At home in Clapham the Redemptorist forces chaplains passed through the house whenever they were able to return from the front. June 1916 was a busy month for visiting chaplains: Fr. Vassal-Philips C.Ss.R. arrived from the front in Egypt, he would later serve on hospital ships; and Fr. Thomas Bradley C.Ss.R. returned having come through the Battle of Jutland. Fr. Bradley was given some time at Bishop Eton before he returned to his ship, and who could begrudge him that, Jutland had been so awful. Fr. John ensure that the men had what they needed and kept in regular communication with them when possible.

Often he would simply receive a telegram informing him that such a Father was safe. He continued in his ministry making provincial visitations and giving retreats. On Christmas Day 1916 the community did not offer Midnight Mass because the lighting restrictions, laid down due to the persistent air raids, made things too difficult. The first Mass of Christmas was celebrated at 5.30am. 1917 began with an intense cold, which may have been an indication of things to come. On 21st July 1917 came the news that Fr. Howard C.Ss.R. had been wounded on the front line and five days later news arrived at Bishop Eton of the death of Fr. Charles Watson C.Ss.R. who was killed in action. On 24th Dec 1917 Fr. John received notification that Fr. Bernard Kavanagh C.Ss.R. had been killed in action, in fact he was shot by a sniper while giving the Last Sacraments to a dying soldier. The scale of these events must have taken their toll on Fr. John and yet when war broke out once more in 1939 he was again Provincial and served the Congregation and those to whom it ministered faithfully during these troubled times.

Fr. John later spent twelve years in South Africa where he was one of the pioneering members of the South African mission working in Heathfield and was expected by many of the clergy to be named Bishop. In 1936 he returned to England but soon began to suffer from arthritis. Indeed, one medical report indicates that he may have had a dislocation of one of his vertebra, which seems to have been incredibly painful and uncomfortable and yet he continued his ministry without complaint. He struggled with sciatica and at the age of 80 he endured two facial operations to remove a malignant growth. He entered the community at Bishop Stortford in 1950 and it soon became clear that his health had deteriorated to such a degree that he was forced to retire from public ministry. In 1961 he celebrated his Diamond Jubilee of Priesthood. Eventually he was missioned to Twyford Abbey, where he was cared for by the Alexian Brothers until he passed away peacefully on the feast of the Nativity of Our Blessed Lady. He was laid to rest at Bishop Stortford on 12th September 1963. He was adored by the younger brethren who enjoyed his stories and who benefitted from his wisdom. We can do no better than finish with their own thoughts about Fr. Charlton:

"We remember him with admiration for his strong and gifted personality, and with affectionate regard for his loyalty as a true son of St. Alphonsus."[408]

Our Mother of Perpetual Succour.

Pray for him.

St. Alphonsus and all our Redemptorist saints.

Pray for us.

VERY REV. FR. JAMES HUGHES C.SS.R.

Born 1878

Professed 1928

Ordained 1904

Died 1950

Fr. Hughes was born in Coatbridge, Scotland, on the 8th August 1878 and desired from a young age to serve the Church in the Sacred Priesthood. He applied to the Archdiocese of Glasgow and was ordained on the 24th May 1904. His first appointment was to be the curate of the parish of St. Aloysius in Glasgow. He had encountered the Redemptorist Fathers Hull, Prime and Jackson C.Ss.R. who had given a mission in his new parish. He was so impressed by these men and saw the blessing of God upon their work: Fr. Hughes had fallen in love with the charism of the Congregation and so, in the early years of his priesthood, he discerned a vocation to be a Redemptorist. The first step was to enquire of Fr. Hull if he might make an application to enter the Congregation However, after some consideration, Fr. Hughes felt that he could not in good conscience ask to be dispensed so quickly from his oath to serve the Archdiocese of Glasgow and after being educated at the expense of the Archdiocese and therefore resolved to think on it no further. In fact, twenty years would go by before the desire to enter the Congregation once again took hold of his heart.

In 1924 Fr. Hughes travelled to a lonely island of the Outer Hebrides to allow the resident priest a holiday. Like the Desert Fathers he spent his days on the island in solitude, making a retreat, and was not long there when the inspiration to become a Redemptorist came over him once more, even more insistent than before and he notes that it became for him an "obsession"[409]. So inclined, he began to read every article he could find concerning the congregation and its saints and became imbued with the spirit of St. Alphonsus and the desire to bring the good news of plentiful redemption to the poor and most abandoned: "I then was inspired to pray, and did pray much that Our Lord through the intercession of St. Alphonsus, St. Clement and St. Gerard, might give me a true vocation to be a Redemptorist."[410] He offered the Holy Sacrifice of the Mass frequently for this intention and gave thanks for the Redemptorist saints in Heaven.

Returning to Glasgow he took these desires to his confessor, who told him that he was convinced that God had answered his prayers and given him a vocation. Fortified by this acknowledgement Fr. Hughes travelled to see his Seminary Professor who, convinced of the truth of this calling, went to the Archbishop to present to him the situation and ensure that Fr. Hughes might be allowed to test his vocation. His Grace was most generous and forwarded to the Congregation this request along with his own recommendation saying that after twenty years faithful service to the Archdiocese he fully supported the application.

Being anxious to enter the novitiate as soon as possible, he wrote to the Holy Father for dispensation from his oath to the diocese. Receiving his dispensation and with the support of his Archbishop and indeed the Congregation he was accepted to enter the Congregation and sent to the Novitiate in Kinnoul, Perth. His Novitiate began on 20th November 1924 under Fr. William Haig C.Ss.R. who served as Novice Master at the time.

The following year, having completed his novitiate he was professed, making vows of poverty, chastity and obedience and the fourth vow and oath of perseverance particular to the Congregation. After three years he was finally professed in Erdington Abbey, Birmingham, on 21st November 1928, following his second Novitiate under Fr. Upton C.Ss.R. In April 1929, he was missioned to South Africa and was appointed Consulter to the community at Diep River, Cape Province, in 1930. In 1933 he was elected Rector of the house at Pretoria for one term of three years. Upon completing this term of office he was brought back to England and served as Provincial from 1936 for two terms, he was succeeded by Fr. John Charlton C.Ss.R. He was exceedingly busy during his time as Provincial and gave a number of retreats and missions to the Redemptorist students as well as to the wider clergy and to nuns. It was Fr. Hughes who accepted the new foundation at Machynlleth, in the Diocese of Menevia in Wales. In 1939 upon the outbreak of the Second World War he sought volunteers to serve as chaplains to the forces and accepted 21 men to be sent. Serving as Provincial he coordinated with his men at the front, ensuring they had what they needed. He also ensure that the

chaplains of the London Area received a monthly retreat in the house in Clapham.

Following the end of his second term as Provincial he was sent to Kinnoul and in 1947 was moved to Erdington Abbey. His final appointment was to Clapham as Provincial Consultor on 1st July 1950. Only four days later he complained of a sharp pain and took some medication. He assisted at several Masses and said Mass himself that morning and when asked at 11.30am how he felt, he replied that he felt no pain. Half an hour later, coming into the garden, Fr. Upton was called over by some workmen who told him one of the Fathers had collapsed on the garden path. It was Father Hughes and it was clear that he had died. Fr. Upton gave him absolution and when Fr. McNulty arrived

With the Holy Oils, Fr. Hughes was anointed and given the Last Blessing. The doctor told the community that he had suffered from a thrombosis and said he must have died in seconds. The following Friday his body was received into the church and the brethren said the Office for the Dead. A Solemn Requiem Mass was sung the next morning by Fr. Provincial and Fr. Hughes was laid to rest. He was known as a kind man, who loved the Redemptorist vocation.

Our Mother of Perpetual Succour.

Pray for him.

St. Alphonsus and all our Redemptorist saints.

Pray for us.

AFTERWORD: REMEMBRANCE & RENEWAL

The Congregation of the Most Holy Redeemer, begun by St. Alphonsus M. de Liguori in Naples was not 200 years old at the outbreak of the First World War and yet the Congregation had already spread throughout the world. The London Province had been established, from Belgium by Fr. De Heeld C.Ss.R., as the English Province in 1843. The Redemptorists began in Plymouth and moved to London taking up residence in Clapham Common and it is hard now to imagine Clapham as it would have looked then. Although it was the Redemptorists who commissioned the building of the church of Our Immaculate Lady of Victories, more commonly known these days as St. Mary's, the congregation did not run the parish initially and a secular priest, who went on to serve as a forces chaplain himself in the Crimean War, was called upon to be the parish priest. A plaque in the church, which is now near the main door, commemorates his proud service to the church and his country. Here we have focussed on the priests of the order who served as chaplains but others sacrificed and others served in incredible ways. We remember with gratitude the example of Fr. John Milcz C.Ss.R. who was a member of the London Province and an inspiration to all who encountered him. He was taken from his home by German soldiers at the age of 14 and was carried off into forced labour. He did not see his family for many years but kept his faith and at the end of his ordeal and after serving in both the

Polish and British Armies after his release, he joined the Redemptorists to serve the poor and most abandoned.

In this little book we have followed in the footsteps of the Redemptorists who served as chaplains to the armed forces. In the refectory of the monastery in Clapham there hangs the list of all the members of the province who went before us. It is a daily reminder that we stand, as it were, on the shoulders of giants! I noticed that three names indicated that these priests had served as chaplains to the armed forces and so I enquired among my superiors to see whether I might be allowed access to the archives to write a small pamphlet on these men in time for the centenary of the end of the First World War in 2018. I soon realised how naïve I had been and as I read letters, which probably had not been seen in nearly 100 years, it became obvious that there were far more chaplains than I had thought. This begged the question: "Do I try and write about all of them or keep to a select few?" To me at least they are heroes, and for that view I make no apology, and I was loathe to miss anyone out.

However I soon realised how long it would take to write about them all, there are around 40 as things stand and I fear there may still be some I have yet to find. In any case, settling on seven chaplains as well as the three men who served as provincial during the two wars I set out to research them and spent many long but enjoyable hours in the archives in Clapham going through files and reading papers. The response of the Redemptorists of the London Province to the news that we were at war showed the power of the living of an authentic religious life. To illustrate my point I will call upon a German Redemptorist, Rev. Fr. Bernard Häring C.Ss.R., who served with distinction as a chaplain to the German army. Fr. Bernard said that the Redemptorist of the future should be free for God, which they live out according to vows of poverty, chastity, obedience and persevearence. The Redemptorists were asked to provide chaplains for the Army and the  Navy by the Cardinal Archbishop of Westminster and rose to the challenge immediately. Of course there were volunteers but those who went were sent.

Some of the chaplains were sent to far off places and saw service in whole range of environments from North Africa and India to Iceland and Central Europe.

Their lives may well have seemed glamorous to the men who were left behind but this is far from the truth. Three Redemptorists never came back from the front line and others were taken as prisoners of war. All of them encountered hardships we can only dream of today and hope never to endure ourselves. Still, those who remained at home in the Redemptorist communities of the London Province, got to work doing their bit. The garden was given over to the growing of vegetables and the rearing of hens. The cellar became the air raid shelter and for a time the school. The Brothers kept the house in order and repaired the damage caused by the bombing. They also went out from the house to help our parishioners who fell into difficulty because of the bombing. They endured the London Blitz and the 'Doddle Bug' raids and ensured that evacuated children did

not go without an education or spiritual nourishment while away from home. The community provided the vital service of hosting passing chaplains and giving retreats for men in service. They provided chaplaincy for the Italian Prisoners of War held close by and spoke to them in Italian forging a cheering link home for these soldiers. In short the community left at home became a vital part of ensuring the moral of the district remained high during the war. Clapham would have been far the poorer without the Redemptorists who served the community. These men were true sons of St. Alphonsus, true Redemptorists, bringing the good news of plentiful redemption to the poor and most abandoned.

So, what about those who came afterwards, today chaplains of many denominations work alongside one another in service of the men and women of the armed forces. I recently spent time with the Royal Navy Chaplaincy Service visiting a number of different Naval Bases including: HMS Collingwood, HMS Excellent, HMS Sultan, HMS Raleigh, RNAS Yeovilton and Britannia Royal Naval College as well as making a ship visit to HMS Albion. The chaplaincies were very ecumenical and felt warm and welcoming places. The chaplains were constantly on the move visiting different departments and ensuring they are in regular contact with the officers and ratings on base. The chaplaincy worked together with a charity called 'Aggies'. This charity aims at providing a 'haven' for sailors on base, a place for them to come and relax and receive support in a relaxed atmosphere. The chaplains can often be found in Aggies, usually in the same building as the chaplaincy, not only because of the bacon sandwiches served at the coffee break but to be available to talk to sailors who might not want to approach them directly. This wonderful charity, working with the chaplains, helps to break down many of the barriers that might prevent a sailor from asking for help. An Aggies initiative, 'Story Book Waves', provides a service for sailors whereby they are able to record themselves reading bed time stories to their children so that when they are sent on operations their children have a vital link to mum or dad[411]. Chaplains can still work to-

ROMAN CATHOLIC CHAPLAINS.
B.R.N.C.

The Reverend Father ~	
BENEDICT COUCH, OSB.RN.	1980~1985
PHELIM ROWLAND. R.N.	1985~1986
VINCENT DOCHERTY. R.N.	1986~1988
THOMAS. M. BURNS. SM. RN.	1988~1992
PAUL DONOVAN. R.N.	1992~1995
BENEDICT COUCH.R.N.	1995~1997
DAVID A LACY. R.N.	1997~1998
STEVEN FORSTER. R.N.	1998~2001
DAVID.M.YATES. RN.	2001~2003
SIMON BRADBURY. RN.	2003-2003
DAVID McLEAN. OP.RN.	2003-2005
MARK CASSIDY.R.N.	2005-2007
SIMON BRADBURY. R.N.	2007~2010
DAVID CONROY. R.N.	2010-2012
DAVID McLEAN.OP. R.N.	2012~2014
DAVID M YATES. R.N.	2014 ~ 2016
MICHAEL SHARKEY. QHC. RN.	2016

wards earning their Green Beret, with the Royal Marine Commandos, or their Dolphins, with the Submarine Service and must remain fighting fit throughout their careers. Chaplains for the Royal Navy begin their training at Britannia Royal Naval College in Dartmouth before moving out on operations. Chaplains to the Royal Army Chaplains Department, once they have completed their basic training are sent to the Armed Forces Chaplaincy Centre in Hampshire for further courses of Study and then to their Regiment. Chaplains serving in the Royal Air Force Chaplaincy Branch, formed in 1918, also carry out much of their further training at Amport House in the Tri Service Chaplaincy Centre. While chaplaincy in the Navy may take ministers away on ships for long periods of time, chaplaincy may also be on the front line or in a base, as in the Army and the Air Force. Chaplains still go, unarmed, into desperately dangerous situations to ensure that the nations fighting men and women are fortified with the Sacraments should the worst happen. Like the chaplains of the world wars who innovated 'chapels on wheels' and established the TocH facility to provide a spiritual retreat for soldiers from the front, the work of the chaplaincy with charities such as Aggies continues to show the importance of the chaplain.

Chaplains are now employed as teachers, leading the soldiers, sailors and aircrew in lectures on a range of topics including ethics. Away on operations and at home they are often appointed to be the education officer ensuring that those serving their country have the opportunity to further their education while in service. Whether they are in the chaplaincy, the class room or on the front line their presence is well received and well appreciated by serving men and women. We pray that Priests may continue to offer themselves as chaplains to the forces and that those who have gone before may be remembered with gratitude and affection.

ROLL OF HONOUR

Name	Regiment/Ship
Rev. Fr. Benjamin F. Brazier C.Ss.R.	Royal Army Chaplains Department
Rev. Fr. Bernard Kavanagh C.Ss.R.	Royal Army Chaplains Department
Rev. Fr. Charles Watson C.Ss.R.	Royal Army Chaplains Department
Rev. Fr. David Ahearne C.Ss.R.	Royal Army Chaplains Department
Rev. Fr. Francis Hutton Prime C.Ss.R.	Royal Army Chaplains Department
Rev. Fr. Gerard Costello C.Ss.R.	Royal Naval Chaplaincy Service
Rev. Fr. James Stack C.Ss.R.	Royal Army Chaplains Department
Rev. Fr. John Evans C.Ss.R.	Royal Army Chaplains Department
Rev. Fr. Thomas Bradley C.Ss.R.	Royal Naval Chaplaincy Service
Rev. Fr. William Maram C.Ss.R.	Royal Army Chaplains Department
Rev. Fr. Denis Gibson C.Ss.R.	Royal Army Chaplains Department
Rev. Fr. Edward John Gibson C.Ss.R.	Royal Army Chaplains Department
Rev. Fr. Augustine Teesedale C.Ss.R.	Royal Army Chaplains Department
Rev. Fr. Ralph McNaulty C.Ss.R.	Royal Army Chaplains Department
Rev. Fr. Oliver Conroy C.Ss.R.	RAF Chaplains Branch
Rev. Fr. John Berry C.Ss.R.	Royal Army Chaplains Department
Rev. Fr. John Maddock C.Ss.R.	RAF Chaplains Branch
Rev. Fr. George Francis Drew C.Ss.R.	Royal Army Chaplains Department

Rev. Fr. Keane C.Ss.R.	Royal Army Chaplains Department
Rev. Fr. Oliver Vassall-Phillips C.Ss.R.	Royal Army Chaplains Department
Rev. Fr. Austin McCabe C.Ss.R.	Royal Army Chaplains Department
Rev. Fr. John Howard C.Ss.R.	Royal Army Chaplains Department
Rev. Fr. C. Wright C.Ss.R.	Royal Army Chaplains Department
Rev. Fr. D. J. Bickle C.Ss.R.	Royal Army Chaplains Department
Rev. Fr. Henry Bowes C.Ss.R.	Royal Army Chaplains Department
Rev. Fr. Michael William Boyle C.Ss.R.	Royal Army Chaplains Department
Rev. Fr. John Cheeseman C.Ss.R.	Royal Army Chaplains Department
Rev. Fr. John Howard C.Ss.R.	Royal Army Chaplains Department
Rev. Fr. R.J. Moore C.Ss.R.	Royal Army Chaplains Department
Rev. Fr. G. Dwyer C.Ss.R.	Royal Army Chaplains Department
Rev. Fr. D. McIlvena C.Ss.R.	Royal Army Chaplains Department
Rev. Fr. C. McPhearson C.Ss.R.	Royal Army Chaplains Department
Rev. Fr. John Joseph William Murray C.Ss.R.	Royal Army Chaplains Department
Rev. Fr. Vincent Young C.Ss.R.	Royal Army Chaplains Department
Rev. Fr. Deary C.Ss.R. R.N. V.G.	Royal Army Chaplains Department

BIBLIOGRAPHY

Aggies, Aggie Weston's, <http://www.aggies.org.uk/> [Accessed 22 Feb 2019].

Fr. Bev Ahearn C.Ss.R., Memoirs of Fr. Charlton, <http://www.redemptorists.co.uk/33-who-we-are.html?start=48> [Accessed 22 Feb 2019].

Alphonsus M. de Liguori, Solemnity of St Dr Alphonsus Liguori CSsR in Solemnities <http://www.redemptorists.co.uk/1510-solemnity-of-st-dr-alphonsus-liguori-cssr.html> [Accessed 21 Feb 2019].

Kevin P. Anastas, The American Way of Operational Art: Attrition or Manoeuvre?, in Defence Technical Information Centre <http://www.dtic.mil/dtic/tr/fulltext/u2/a254194.pdf> [Accessed 4 April 2018].

Archives of the Catholic Diocese of Brentwood.

Beaumont Union, Catholic Chaplains in The Great War WW1, in PDFs <http://www.beaumont-union.co.uk/pdfs/CATHOLIC%20CHAPLAINS%20in%20THE%20GREAT%20WAR%20WW1.pdf> [Accessed 4 April 2018].

Winston Churchill, We will all go down fighting to the end: Great Ideas 97 (London: Penguin, 2010).

CSSR PA Bishop Eton, Letter, Evans to Bishop Eton Community 9th November 1914.

CSSR PA London, Domestic Chronicles of Bishop Eton Liverpool.

CSSR PA London, Domestic Chronicles of St Mary's Clapham 1893-1930.

CSSR PA London, Domestic Chronicles of St Mary's Clapham 1931-1956.

CSSR PA London, Fr. David Ahearne C.Ss.R. Biography.

CSSR PA London, Fr. Thomas Bradley C.Ss.R. Biography.

CSSR PA London, Domestic Chronicles of St Mary's Clapham. Biography: Fr. Charlton.

CSSR PA London, Domestic Chronicles of St Mary's Clapham. Biography: Fr. Conroy.

CSSR PA London, Domestic Chronicles of St Mary's Clapham. Biography: Fr. Gibson.

CSSR PA London, Domestic Chronicles of St Mary's Clapham. Biography: Fr. Hughes.

CSSR PA London, Domestic Chronicles of St Mary's Clapham. Biography: Fr. Hull.

CSSR PA London, Domestic Chronicles of St Mary's Clapham. Biography: Fr. Kavanagh.

CSSR PA London, Domestic Chronicles of St Mary's Clapham. Biography: Fr. Watson.

Peter Duckers, British Military Medals: A Guide for the Collector and Family Historian (Barnsley: Pen & Sword, 2013).

FAAOA, Fleet Air Arm History, in Heritage <http://fleetairarmoa.org/fleet-air-arm-history-timeline> [Accessed 4 April 2018].

Mike Farquharson-Roberts, A History of the Royal Navy: World War I (London: I. B. Tauris, 2014).

Norman Ferguson, The First World War: A Miscellany (Chichester: Summersdale Publishers Ltd, 2014).

Carol Glatz, Pope Francis in The Catholic Herald, <https://www.thecatholictelegraph.com/pope-francis-priests-should-be-shepherds-living-with-the-smell-of-the-sheep/13439> [Accessed 21 Feb 2019].

The Gazette, WW1 The Battle of Mons, in The Gazette <https://www.thegazette.co.uk/all-notices/content/218> [Accessed 4 April 2018].

King George VI, The Speech of HM The King 3rd September 1939 in Historic UK, <https://www.historic-uk.com/HistoryUK/HistoryofBritain/The-Kings-Speech/> [Accessed 21 Feb 2019].

James Hagerty, Priests in Uniform: Catholic Chaplains to the British Forces in the First World War (Leominster: Gracewing, 2017).

James Hagerty, Tom Johnstone, The Cross on the Sword: Catholic Chaplains in the Forces (London: Geoffrey Chapman, 1996).

Peter Hart, Nigel Steel, Jutland 1916: Death in the Grey Wastes (London: Cassell Military, 2004).

Max Hastings, Catastrophe: Europe Goes to War 1914 (London: William Collins, 2014).

Horatio Nelson, History's Heroes, <http://historysheroes.e2bn.org/hero/howviewed/5> [Accessed 21 Feb 2019].

Denis McBride, Journeying with Jonah (Chawton: Redemptorist Publications, 2015).

Gerry Murphy, Where did that regiment go? The lineage of British infantry regiments at a glance (Stroud: Spellmount, 2009).

Venerable Joseph Passerat C.Ss.R., Redemptorist Saints, <www.redemptorists.co.uk> [Accessed 21 Feb 2019].

RAF Chaplaincy Branch Archives, Email RE. 2TAF.

RAF Chaplaincy Branch, Overview in RAF Chaplaincy Branch, <https://www.raf.mod.uk/our-organisation/units/raf-chaplains/> [Accessed 21 Feb 2019].

Royal Army Chaplains Department Museum Archives.

Mian Ridge, The Tablet: Interview with Fr. Gerard COstello C.Ss.R. R.M. Dated 5 June 2004.

Ben Walsh, Why did Britain go to War, in Great War <www.nationalarchives.gov.uk/education/greatwar/g2/backgroundcs1.htm> [Accessed 4 April 2018]

REFERENCES

[1] Hagerty, James, Johnstone, Tom, *The Cross on the Sword: Catholic Chaplains in the Forces* (London: Geoffrey Chapman, 1996), p. v.

[2] Royal Army Chaplains Department Museum.

[3] Ibid.

[4] Denis McBride, *Journeying with Jonah* (Chawton: Redemptorist Publications, 2015), pp. 39-42.

[5] Mike Farquharson-Roberts, *A History of the Royal Navy: World War I* (London: I. B. Tauris, 2014), p. 5.

[6] Ibid.

[7] CSSR PA London, Domestic Chronicles of St Mary's Clapham 1893-1930. pp. 275-276.

[8] Ibid.

[9] Norman Ferguson, *The First World War: A Miscellany* (Chichester: Summersdale Publishers Ltd, 2014), p. 26.

[10] CSSR PA London, Domestic Chronicles of St Mary's Clapham 1893-1930. p. 276.

[11] CSSR PA London, Domestic Chronicles of St Mary's Clapham 1893-1930. p. 275.

[12] Max Hastings, *Catastrophe: Europe Goes to War 1914* (London: William Collins, 2014), p. xxxiii.

[13] Hastings, Catastrophe (London: William Collins, 2014), p. xxxii.

[14] Hastings, *Catastrophe* (London: William Collins, 2014), p. xxxix.

[15] Hastings, *Catastrophe* (London: William Collins, 2014), p. 26.

[16] Ben Walsh, Why did Britain go to War, in Great War <www.nationalarchives.gov.uk/education/greatwar/g2/backgroundcs1.htm> [Accessed 4 April 2018].

[17] Ibid.

[18] Hastings, Catastrophe (London: William Collins, 2014), p. xxiv.

[19] Mike Farquharson-Roberts, A History of the Royal Navy: World War I (London: I. B. Tauris, 2014), p. 2.

[20] Kevin P. Anastas, The American Way of Operational Art: Attrition or Manoeuvre?, in Defence Technical Information Centre <http://www.dtic.mil/dtic/tr/fulltext/u2/a254194.pdf> [Accessed 4 April 2018].

[21] Gerry Murphy, *Where did that regiment go? The lineage of British infantry regiments at a glance* (Stroud: Spellmount, 2009), p. 91.

[22] The Gazette, WW1 The Battle of Mons, in The Gazette <https://www.thegazette.co.uk/all-notices/content/218> [Accessed 4 April 2018].

[23] FAAOA, Fleet Air Arm History, in Heritage <http://fleetairarmoa.org/fleet-air-arm-history-timeline> [Accessed 4 April 2018].

[24] CSSR PA London, Domestic Chronicles of St Mary's Clapham 1893-1930. p. 280.

[25] CSSR PA London, Domestic Chronicles of St Mary's Clapham 1893-1930. pp. 281-282.

[26] CSSR PA Bishop Eton, Letter, Evans to Bishop Eton Community 9th November 1914.

[27] CSSR PA London, Domestic Chronicles of St Mary's Clapham 1893-1930. p. 291.

[28] Ibid.

[29] CSSR PA London, Domestic Chronicles of St Mary's Clapham 1893-1930. p. 297.

[30] CSSR PA London, Domestic Chronicles of St Mary's Clapham 1893-1930. p. 298.

[31] Ibid.

[32] Ibid.

[33] Gerry Murphy, Where did that regiment go? The lineage of British infantry regiments at a glance (Stroud: Spellmount, 2009), p. 94.

[34] Hagerty, Johnstone, The Cross on the Sword (London: Geoffrey Chapman, 1996), pp. 106-107.

[35] James Hagerty, *Priests in Uniform: Catholic Chaplains to the British Forces in the First World War* (Leominster: Gracewing, 2017), p. 7.

[36] Hagerty, Johnstone, The Cross on the Sword (London: Geoffrey Chapman, 1996), p. 110.

[37] Hagerty, Johnstone, The Cross on the Sword (London: Geoffrey Chapman, 1996), p. 61

[38] CSSR PA London, Domestic Chronicles of St Mary's Clapham 1893-1930. p.

304.

[39] CSSR PA London, Domestic Chronicles of St Mary's Clapham 1893-1930. p. 308.

[40] CSSR PA London, Domestic Chronicles of St Mary's Clapham 1893-1930. p. 310.

[41] CSSR PA London, Domestic Chronicles of St Mary's Clapham 1893-1930. p. 311.

[42] CSSR PA London, Domestic Chronicles of St Mary's Clapham 1893-1930. p. 312.

[43] CSSR PA London, Domestic Chronicles of St Mary's Clapham 1893-1930. p. 324.

[44] CSSR PA London, Domestic Chronicles of St Mary's Clapham 1893-1930. p. 328.

[45] Ibid.

[46] Norman Ferguson, *The First World War: A Miscellany* (Chichester: Summersdale Publishers Ltd, 2014), pp. 100-101.

[47] CSSR PA London, Domestic Chronicles of St Mary's Clapham 1893-1930. p. 329.

[48] CSSR PA London, Domestic Chronicles of St Mary's Clapham 1893-1930. p. 338.

[49] Peter Duckers, *British Military Medals: A Guide for the Collector and Family Historian* (Barnsley: Pen & Sword, 2013), pp.145-146.

[50] CSSR PA London, Domestic Chronicles of St Mary's Clapham 1893-1930. p. 340.

[51] CSSR PA London, Domestic Chronicles of St Mary's Clapham 1893-1930. p. 346.

[52] CSSR PA London, Domestic Chronicles of St Mary's Clapham 1893-1930. p. 347.

[53] Ibid.

[54] CSSR PA London, Domestic Chronicles of St Mary's Clapham 1893-1930. p. 355.

[55] CSSR PA London, Domestic Chronicles of St Mary's Clapham 1893-1930. p. 356.

[56] CSSR PA London, Domestic Chronicles of St Mary's Clapham 1893-1930. p. 357.

[57] Ibid.

[58] Hagerty, Priests in Uniform (Leominster: Gracewing, 2017), p.8.

[59] CSSR PA London, Domestic Chronicles of St Mary's Clapham 1893-1930. p. 364.

[60] CSSR PA London, Domestic Chronicles of St Mary's Clapham 1893-1930. p. 363.

[61] CSSR PA London, Domestic Chronicles of St Mary's Clapham 1893-1930. p. 363.

[62] CSSR PA London, Domestic Chronicles of St Mary's Clapham 1893-1930. p. 366.

[63] Peter Duckers, British Military Medals: A Guide for the Collector and Family Historian (Barnsley: Pen & Sword, 2013), p. 128.

[64] CSSR PA London, Domestic Chronicles of St Mary's Clapham 1893-1930. p. 371.

[65] Ibid.

[66] CSSR PA London, Domestic Chronicles of St Mary's Clapham 1893-1930. p. 372.

[67] CSSR PA London, Domestic Chronicles of St Mary's Clapham 1893-1930. p. 372.

[68] Ibid.

[69] CSSR PA London, Domestic Chronicles of St Mary's Clapham 1893-1930. p. 373.

[70] CSSR PA London, Domestic Chronicles of St Mary's Clapham 1893-1930. p. 387.

[71] CSSR PA London, Domestic Chronicles of St Mary's Clapham 1893-1930. p. 389.

[72] CSSR PA London, Domestic Chronicles of St Mary's Clapham 1893-1930. p. 389.

[73] Ibid.

[74] CSSR PA London, Domestic Chronicles of St Mary's Clapham 1893-1930. p. 392.

[75] CSSR PA London, Domestic Chronicles of St Mary's Clapham 1893-1930. p. 392.

[76] CSSR PA London, Domestic Chronicles of St Mary's Clapham 1893-1930. p. 392.

[77] CSSR PA London, Domestic Chronicles of St Mary's Clapham 1893-1930. p. 393.

[78] CSSR PA London, Domestic Chronicles of St Mary's Clapham 1893-1930. p. 395.

[79] CSSR PA London, Domestic Chronicles of St Mary's Clapham 1893-1930. p. 399.

[80] Ibid.

[81] CSSR PA London, Domestic Chronicles of St Mary's Clapham 1893-1930. p.

399.

[82] Beaumont Union, Catholic Chaplains in The Great War WW1, in PDFs <http://www.beaumont-union.co.uk/pdfs/CATHOLIC%20CHAPLAINS%20in%20THE%20GREAT%20WAR%20WW1.pdf> [Accessed 4 April 2018].

[83] Hastings, *Catastrophe* (London: William Collins, 2013), p.563.

[84] Ferguson, Norman, *The Second World War: A Miscellany* (Chichester: Summersdale Publishers Ltd, 2014), p.11.

[85] Ibid.

[86] Ferguson, *The Second World War* (Chichester: Summersdale Publishers Ltd, 2014), p.12.

[87] King George VI, The Speech of HM The King 3rd September 1939 in Historic UK, <https://www.historic-uk.com/HistoryUK/HistoryofBritain/The-Kings-Speech/> [Accessed 21 Feb 2019].

[88] CSSR PA London, Domestic Chronicles of St Mary's Clapham 1931-1956, entry: 15 Feb 1939.

[89] CSSR PA London, Domestic Chronicles of St Mary's Clapham 1931-1956, entry: 26 Feb 1939.

[90] CSSR PA London, Domestic Chronicles of St Mary's Clapham 1931-1956, entry: 11 Mar 1939.

[91] CSSR PA London, Domestic Chronicles of St Mary's Clapham 1931-1956, entry: 12 Mar 1939.

[92] CSSR PA London, Domestic Chronicles of St Mary's Clapham 1931-1956, entry: 28 May 1939.

[93] CSSR PA London, Domestic Chronicles of St Mary's Clapham 1931-1956, entry: 28 May 1939.

[94] Ibid.

[95] CSSR PA London, Domestic Chronicles of St Mary's Clapham 1931-1956, entry: 28 May 1939.

[96] CSSR PA London, Domestic Chronicles of St Mary's Clapham 1931-1956, entry: 7th July 1939.

[97] CSSR PA London, Domestic Chronicles of St Mary's Clapham 1931-1956, entry: 25 Aug 1939.

[98] CSSR PA London, Domestic Chronicles of St Mary's Clapham 1931-1956, entry: 3 Sept 1939.

[99] CSSR PA London, Domestic Chronicles of St Mary's Clapham 1931-1956, entry: 6 Sept 1939.

[100] Archives of the Catholic Diocese of Brentwood.

[101] CSSR PA London, Domestic Chronicles of St Mary's Clapham 1931-1956, entry: 6 Sept 1939.

[102] CSSR PA London, Domestic Chronicles of St Mary's Clapham 1931-1956, entry: 6 Oct 1939.

[103] CSSR PA London, Domestic Chronicles of St Mary's Clapham 1931-1956, entry: 1 Nov 1939.

[104] CSSR PA London, Domestic Chronicles of St Mary's Clapham 1931-1956, entry: 12 Nov 1939.

[105] CSSR PA London, Domestic Chronicles of St Mary's Clapham 1931-1956, entry: 24 Nov 1939.

[106] CSSR PA London, Domestic Chronicles of St Mary's Clapham 1931-1956, entry: 7 Dec 1939.

[107] CSSR PA London, Domestic Chronicles of St Mary's Clapham 1931-1956, entry: 11 Dec 1939.

[108] Ibid.

[109] CSSR PA London, Domestic Chronicles of St Mary's Clapham 1931-1956, entry: 13 Mar 1940.

[110] CSSR PA London, Domestic Chronicles of St Mary's Clapham 1931-1956, entry: 22 Mar 1940.

[111] CSSR PA London, Domestic Chronicles of St Mary's Clapham 1931-1956, entry: 24 May 1940.

[112] CSSR PA London, Domestic Chronicles of St Mary's Clapham 1931-1956, entry: 28 May 1940.

[113] CSSR PA London, Domestic Chronicles of St Mary's Clapham 1931-1956, entry: 31 May 1940.

[114] CSSR PA London, Domestic Chronicles of St Mary's Clapham 1931-1956, entry: 6 Jun 1940.

[115] CSSR PA London, Domestic Chronicles of St Mary's Clapham 1931-1956, entry: 10 Jun 1940.

[116] CSSR PA London, Domestic Chronicles of St Mary's Clapham 1931-1956, entry: 13 Jun 1940.

[117] CSSR PA London, Domestic Chronicles of St Mary's Clapham 1931-1956, entry: 20 Jun 1940.

[118] CSSR PA London, Domestic Chronicles of St Mary's Clapham 1931-1956, entry: 25 Jun 1940.

[119] CSSR PA London, Domestic Chronicles of St Mary's Clapham 1931-1956, entry: 30 Jul 1940.

[120] CSSR PA London, Domestic Chronicles of St Mary's Clapham 1931-1956, entry: 22 Oct 1941.

[121] CSSR PA London, Domestic Chronicles of St Mary's Clapham 1931-1956, entry: 23 Oct 1941.

[122] CSSR PA London, Domestic Chronicles of St Mary's Clapham 1931-1956, entry: 7 Nov 1941.

[123] CSSR PA London, Domestic Chronicles of St Mary's Clapham 1931-1956, entry: 9 Nov 1941.

[124] Ibid.

[125] CSSR PA London, Domestic Chronicles of St Mary's Clapham 1931-1956, entry: 10 Nov 1941.

[126] CSSR PA London, Domestic Chronicles of St Mary's Clapham 1931-1956, entry: 4 Dec 1941.

[127] CSSR PA London, Domestic Chronicles of St Mary's Clapham 1931-1956, entry: 8 Dec 1941.

[128] CSSR PA London, Domestic Chronicles of St Mary's Clapham 1931-1956, entry: 28 Aug 1942.

[129] CSSR PA London, Domestic Chronicles of St Mary's Clapham 1931-1956, entry: 28 Aug 1942.

[130] CSSR PA London, Domestic Chronicles of St Mary's Clapham 1931-1956, entry: 6 Nov 1942.

[131] CSSR PA London, Domestic Chronicles of St Mary's Clapham 1931-1956, entry: 11 Nov 1942.

[132] CSSR PA London, Domestic Chronicles of St Mary's Clapham 1931-1956, entry: 13 Nov 1942.

[133] CSSR PA London, Domestic Chronicles of St Mary's Clapham 1931-1956, entry: 15 Jun 1942.

[134] CSSR PA London, Domestic Chronicles of St Mary's Clapham 1931-1956, entry: 24 Dec 1942.

[135] CSSR PA London, Domestic Chronicles of St Mary's Clapham 1931-1956, entry: 31 Dec 1942.

[136] CSSR PA London, Domestic Chronicles of St Mary's Clapham 1931-1956, entry: 15 Jul 1943.

[137] CSSR PA London, Domestic Chronicles of St Mary's Clapham 1931-1956, entry: 26th Aug 1943.

[138] CSSR PA London, Domestic Chronicles of St Mary's Clapham 1931-1956, entry: 28 Aug 1943.

[139] CSSR PA London, Domestic Chronicles of St Mary's Clapham 1931-1956, entry: 3 Sept 1943.

[140] CSSR PA London, Domestic Chronicles of St Mary's Clapham 1931-1956, entry: 7 Sept 1943.

[141] CSSR PA London, Domestic Chronicles of St Mary's Clapham 1931-1956, entry: 8 Sept 1943.

[142] CSSR PA London, Domestic Chronicles of St Mary's Clapham 1931-1956, entry: 18 Oct 1943.

[143] CSSR PA London, Domestic Chronicles of St Mary's Clapham 1931-1956, entry: 6 Mar 1944.

[144] CSSR PA London, Domestic Chronicles of St Mary's Clapham 1931-1956, entry: 16 Mar 1944.

[145] CSSR PA London, Domestic Chronicles of St Mary's Clapham 1931-1956, entry: 22 Mar 1944.

[146] CSSR PA London, Domestic Chronicles of St Mary's Clapham 1931-1956, entry: 5 June 1944.

[147] CSSR PA London, Domestic Chronicles of St Mary's Clapham 1931-1956, entry: 6 Jun 1944.

[148] CSSR PA London, Domestic Chronicles of St Mary's Clapham 1931-1956, entry: 8-13 Jun 1944.

[149] CSSR PA London, Domestic Chronicles of St Mary's Clapham 1931-1956, entry: 15 Jun 1944.

[150] CSSR PA London, Domestic Chronicles of St Mary's Clapham 1931-1956, entry: 17 Jun 1944.

[151] CSSR PA London, Domestic Chronicles of St Mary's Clapham 1931-1956, entry: 18 Jun 1944.

[152] CSSR PA London, Domestic Chronicles of St Mary's Clapham 1931-1956, entry: Jul 1944.

[153] CSSR PA London, Domestic Chronicles of St Mary's Clapham 1931-1956, entry: 1 Aug 1944.

[154] CSSR PA London, Domestic Chronicles of St Mary's Clapham 1931-1956, entry: 28 Oct 1944.

[155] CSSR PA London, Domestic Chronicles of St Mary's Clapham 1931-1956, entry: 29 Nov 1944.

[156] CSSR PA London, Domestic Chronicles of St Mary's Clapham 1931-1956, entry: 7 Mar 1945.

[157] CSSR PA London, Domestic Chronicles of St Mary's Clapham 1931-1956, entry: 5 May 1945.

[158] CSSR PA London, Domestic Chronicles of St Mary's Clapham 1931-1956, entry: 8 May 1945.

[159] CSSR PA London, Domestic Chronicles of St Mary's Clapham 1931-1956, entry: 26 May 1945.

[160] CSSR PA London, Domestic Chronicles of St Mary's Clapham 1931-1956, entry: 1 Aug 1945.

[161] CSSR PA London, Fr. David Ahearne C.Ss.R. Biography.

[162] CSSR PA London, Fr. David Ahearne C.Ss.R. Letter from Bishop.

[163] Ibid.

[164] Ibid.

[165] CSSR PA London, Fr. David Ahearne C.Ss.R. Biography.

[166] Ibid.

[167] Ibid.

[168] CSSR PA London, Fr. David Ahearne C.Ss.R. Biography.

[169] Ibid.

[170] CSSR PA London, Fr. David Ahearne C.Ss.R. Biography.

[171] Ibid.

[172] Ibid.

[173] Ibid.

[174] CSSR PA London, Fr. David Ahearne C.Ss.R. Letter.

[175] Carol Glatz, Pope Francis in The Catholic Herald, <https://www.thecatholictelegraph.com/pope-francis-priests-should-be-shepherds-living-with-the-smell-of-the-sheep/13439> [Accessed 21 Feb 2019].

[176] CSSR PA London, Fr. David Ahearne C.Ss.R. Biography.

[177] CSSR PA London, Fr. David Ahearne C.Ss.R. Biography.

[178] CSSR PA London, Fr. David Ahearne C.Ss.R. Biography.

[179] Ibid.

[180] CSSR PA London, Fr. David Ahearne C.Ss.R. Biography.

[181] CSSR PA London, Fr. David Ahearne C.Ss.R. Biography.

[182] CSSR PA London, Fr. Thomas Bradley C.Ss.R. Biography.

[183] CSSR PA London, Fr. Thomas Bradley C.Ss.R. Biography.

[184] CSSR PA London, Fr. Thomas Bradley C.Ss.R. Biography.

[185] Alphonsus M. de Liguori, Solemnity of St Dr Alphonsus Liguori CSsR in Solemnities <http://www.redemptorists.co.uk/1510-solemnity-of-st-dr-alphonsus-liguori-cssr.html> [Accessed 21 Feb 2019].

[186] CSSR PA London, Fr. Thomas Bradley C.Ss.R. Biography.

[187] Ibid.

[188] Hagerty, James, Johnstone, Tom, The Cross on the Sword: Catholic Chaplains in the Forces (London: Geoffrey Chapman, 1996), pp. 51-52.

[189] CSSR PA London, Domestic Chronicles of St Mary's Clapham, entry: 19 Dec 1914.

[190] CSSR PA London, Domestic Chronicles of St Mary's Clapham, entry: 24 Nov

1914.

[191] Hagerty, James, Johnstone, Tom, *The Cross on the Sword: Catholic Chaplains in the Forces* (London: Geoffrey Chapman, 1996), p. 61.

[192] Hagerty, James, Johnstone, Tom, *The Cross on the Sword: Catholic Chaplains in the Forces* (London: Geoffrey Chapman, 1996), p. 61.

[193]

[194] Hagerty, James, Johnstone, Tom, *The Cross on the Sword: Catholic Chaplains in the Forces* (London: Geoffrey Chapman, 1996), p. 61.

[195] Ibid.

[196] CSSR PA London, Fr. Thomas Bradley C.Ss.R. Article in Clapham Observer.

[197] Hagerty, James, Johnstone, Tom, *The Cross on the Sword: Catholic Chaplains in the Forces* (London: Geoffrey Chapman, 1996), p. 52.

[198] Hagerty, James, Johnstone, Tom, *The Cross on the Sword: Catholic Chaplains in the Forces* (London: Geoffrey Chapman, 1996), p. 64.

[199] CSSR PA London, Domestic Chronicles of St Mary's Clapham, entry: 31 May 1916.

[200] Hart, Peter, Steel, Nigel, *Jutland 1916: Death in the Grey Wastes* (London: Cassell Military, 2004), p. 419.

[201] CSSR PA London, Domestic Chronicles of St Mary's Clapham.

[202] Hagerty, James, Johnstone, Tom, *The Cross on the Sword: Catholic Chaplains in the Forces* (London: Geoffrey Chapman, 1996), p. 65.

[203] Hart, Peter, Steel, Nigel, *Jutland 1916: Death in the Grey Wastes* (London: Cassell Military, 2004), pp. 86-87.

[204] Hart, Peter, Steel, Nigel, *Jutland 1916: Death in the Grey Wastes* (London: Cassell Military, 2004), p. 87.

[205] Hagerty, James, Johnstone, Tom, *The Cross on the Sword: Catholic Chaplains in the Forces* (London: Geoffrey Chapman, 1996), p. 64.

[206] Hart, Peter, Steel, Nigel, *Jutland 1916: Death in the Grey Wastes* (London: Cassell Military, 2004), p. 118.

[207] Hart, Peter, Steel, Nigel, *Jutland 1916: Death in the Grey Wastes* (London: Cassell Military, 2004), p. 118.

[208] Hart, Peter, Steel, Nigel, *Jutland 1916: Death in the Grey Wastes* (London: Cassell Military, 2004), p. 118.

[209] Hart, Peter, Steel, Nigel, *Jutland 1916: Death in the Grey Wastes* (London: Cassell Military, 2004), p. 292.

[210] Ibid.

[211] Hart, Peter, Steel, Nigel, *Jutland 1916: Death in the Grey Wastes* (London: Cassell Military, 2004), p. 406.

[212] CSSR PA London, Domestic Chronicles of St Mary's Clapham. Letter from

Superior General C.Ss.R.

[213] CSSR PA London, Domestic Chronicles of St Mary's Clapham. Entry: 11 November 1918.

[214] CSSR PA London, Domestic Chronicles of St Mary's Clapham. Letter from Cardinal.

[215] King George VI, The Speech of HM The King 3rd September 1939 in Historic UK, <https://www.historic-uk.com/HistoryUK/HistoryofBritain/The-Kings-Speech/> [Accessed 21 Feb 2019].

[216] CSSR PA London, Domestic Chronicles of St Mary's Clapham. Entry: 28 May 1939.

[217] CSSR PA London, Domestic Chronicles of St Mary's Clapham. Entry: 28 May 1939.

[218] CSSR PA London, Domestic Chronicles of St Mary's Clapham. Entry: 3 September 1939.

[219] CSSR PA London, Domestic Chronicles of St Mary's Clapham. Letter from Fr. Bradley.

[220] CSSR PA London, Domestic Chronicles of St Mary's Clapham. Letter from Fr. Bradley.

[221] Ibid.

[222] CSSR PA London, Domestic Chronicles of St Mary's Clapham. Letter from Fr. Bradley.

[223] Ibid.

[224] CSSR PA London, Domestic Chronicles of St Mary's Clapham. Letter from Fr. Bradley.

[225] CSSR PA London, Domestic Chronicles of St Mary's Clapham. Letter from Fr. Bradley.

[226] Ibid.

[227] CSSR PA London, Domestic Chronicles of St Mary's Clapham. Letter from Fr. Bradley.

[228] CSSR PA London, Domestic Chronicles of St Mary's Clapham. Letter from The Admiralty.

[229] CSSR PA London, Domestic Chronicles of St Mary's Clapham. Letter from Fr. Provincial.

[230] CSSR PA London, Domestic Chronicles of St Mary's Clapham. Letter from The Admiralty.

[231] CSSR PA London, Domestic Chronicles of St Mary's Clapham. Letter from Fr. Provincial.

[232] CSSR PA London, Domestic Chronicles of St Mary's Clapham. Letter from Archbishop Leo of Mauritius.

[233] CSSR PA London, Domestic Chronicles of St Mary's Clapham. Sermon of Fr. Prime on Fr. Bradley.

[234] CSSR PA London, Domestic Chronicles of St Mary's Clapham. Letter from Senior Naval Chaplain.

[235] CSSR PA London, Domestic Chronicles of St Mary's Clapham. Biography: Fr. Bradley.

[236] Horatio Nelson, History's Heroes, <http://historysheroes.e2bn.org/hero/howviewed/5> [Accessed 21 Feb 2019].

[237] CSSR PA London, Domestic Chronicles of St Mary's Clapham. Letter from Senior Naval Chaplain.

[238] CSSR PA London, Domestic Chronicles of St Mary's Clapham. Letter from Fr. Costello.

[239] CSSR PA London, Domestic Chronicles of St Mary's Clapham. Report of the Prefect of Students.

[240] Ibid.

[241] CSSR PA London, Domestic Chronicles of St Mary's Clapham.

[242] Winston Churchill, We will all go down fighting to the end: Great Ideas 97 (London: Penguin, 2010), pp. 112-113.

[243] CSSR PA London, Domestic Chronicles of St Mary's Clapham. Interview Article: The Tablet.

[244] CSSR PA London, Domestic Chronicles of St Mary's Clapham. Interview Article: The Tablet.

[245] CSSR PA London, Domestic Chronicles of St Mary's Clapham. Interview Article: The Tablet.

[246] CSSR PA London, Domestic Chronicles of St Mary's Clapham. Interview Article: The Tablet.

[247] CSSR PA London, Domestic Chronicles of St Mary's Clapham. Interview Article: The Tablet.

[248] Ibid.

[249] CSSR PA London, Domestic Chronicles of St Mary's Clapham. Interview Article: The Tablet.

[250] Ibid.

[251] CSSR PA London, Domestic Chronicles of St Mary's Clapham. Interview Article: The Tablet.

[252] CSSR PA London, Domestic Chronicles of St Mary's Clapham. Interview Article: The Tablet.

[253] CSSR PA London, Domestic Chronicles of St Mary's Clapham. Interview Article: The Tablet.

[254] Ibid.

[255] CSSR PA London, Domestic Chronicles of St Mary's Clapham. Interview Article: The Tablet.

[256] Ibid.

[257] CSSR PA London, Domestic Chronicles of St Mary's Clapham. Interview Article: The Tablet.

[258] Ibid.

[259] CSSR PA London, Domestic Chronicles of St Mary's Clapham. Letter.

[260] CSSR PA London, Domestic Chronicles of St Mary's Clapham. Interview Article: The Tablet.

[261] CSSR PA London, Domestic Chronicles of St Mary's Clapham. Letter from Brigadier Leicester.

[262] Ibid.

[263] CSSR PA London, Domestic Chronicles of St Mary's Clapham. Letter from Brigadier Leicester.

[264] CSSR PA London, Domestic Chronicles of St Mary's Clapham. Letter from Brigadier Leicester.

[265] Ibid.

[266] CSSR PA London, Domestic Chronicles of St Mary's Clapham. Letter from Fr. Costello.

[267] CSSR PA London, Domestic Chronicles of St Mary's Clapham. Letter from Superior General.

[268] CSSR PA London, Domestic Chronicles of St Mary's Clapham. Biography: Fr. Watson.

[269] Ibid.

[270] CSSR PA London, Domestic Chronicles of St Mary's Clapham. Biography: Fr. Watson.

[271] CSSR PA London, Domestic Chronicles of St Mary's Clapham. Biography: Fr. Watson.

[272] Ibid.

[273] CSSR PA London, Domestic Chronicles of St Mary's Clapham. Biography: Fr. Watson.

[274] CSSR PA London, Domestic Chronicles of St Mary's Clapham. Biography: Fr. Watson.

[275] CSSR PA London, Domestic Chronicles of St Mary's Clapham. Biography: Fr. Watson.

[276] Ibid.

[277] CSSR PA London, Domestic Chronicles of St Mary's Clapham. Biography: Fr. Watson.

[278] CSSR PA London, Domestic Chronicles of St Mary's Clapham. Biography: Fr. Watson.

[279] Ibid.

[280] CSSR PA London, Domestic Chronicles of St Mary's Clapham. Biography: Fr. Watson.

[281] CSSR PA London, Domestic Chronicles of St Mary's Clapham. Biography: Fr. Watson.

[282] CSSR PA London, Domestic Chronicles of St Mary's Clapham. Biography: Fr. Watson.

[283] CSSR PA London, Domestic Chronicles of St Mary's Clapham. Biography: Fr. Watson.

[284] CSSR PA London, Domestic Chronicles of St Mary's Clapham. Biography: Fr. Watson.

[285] Ibid.

[286] CSSR PA London, Domestic Chronicles of St Mary's Clapham. Biography: Fr. Watson.

[287] CSSR PA London, Domestic Chronicles of St Mary's Clapham. Biography: Fr. Watson.

[288] CSSR PA London, Domestic Chronicles of St Mary's Clapham. Biography: Fr. Watson.

[289] CSSR PA London, Domestic Chronicles of St Mary's Clapham. Biography: Fr. Watson.

[290] CSSR PA London, Domestic Chronicles of St Mary's Clapham. Biography: Fr. Watson.

[291] CSSR PA London, Domestic Chronicles of St Mary's Clapham. Biography: Fr. Watson.

[292] CSSR PA London, Domestic Chronicles of St Mary's Clapham. Biography: Fr. Watson.

[293] CSSR PA London, Domestic Chronicles of St Mary's Clapham. Biography: Fr. Watson.

[294] CSSR PA London, Domestic Chronicles of St Mary's Clapham. Biography: Fr. Watson.

[295] CSSR PA London, Domestic Chronicles of St Mary's Clapham. Biography: Fr. Watson.

[296] CSSR PA London, Domestic Chronicles of St Mary's Clapham. Biography: Fr. Watson.

[297] CSSR PA London, Domestic Chronicles of St Mary's Clapham. Biography: Fr. Watson.

[298] CSSR PA London, Domestic Chronicles of St Mary's Clapham. Biography: Fr.

Watson.

[299] Ibid.

[300] CSSR PA London, Domestic Chronicles of St Mary's Clapham. Biography: Fr. Watson.

[301] Ibid.

[302] CSSR PA London, Domestic Chronicles of St Mary's Clapham. Entry: 21 Feb 1916.

[303] CSSR PA London, Domestic Chronicles of St Mary's Clapham. Entry: 20 Nov 1916.

[304] CSSR PA London, Domestic Chronicles of St Mary's Clapham. Entry: 17 Mar 1917.

[305] CSSR PA London, Domestic Chronicles of St Mary's Clapham. Entry: 26 Jul 1918.

[306] CSSR PA London, Domestic Chronicles of St Mary's Clapham.

[307] CSSR PA London, Domestic Chronicles of St Mary's Clapham. Letter.

[308] CSSR PA London, Domestic Chronicles of St Mary's Clapham. Letter from Fr. P.Deeley C.F.

[309] CSSR PA London, Domestic Chronicles of St Mary's Clapham. Record of Burial Commonwealth War Graves Commision.

[310] CSSR PA London, Domestic Chronicles of St Mary's Clapham. Biography: Fr. Watson.

[311] CSSR PA London, Domestic Chronicles of St Mary's Clapham. Letter from Fr. P.Deeley C.F.

[312] CSSR PA London, Domestic Chronicles of St Mary's Clapham. Biography: Fr. Kavanagh.

[313] CSSR PA London, Domestic Chronicles of St Mary's Clapham. Biography: Fr. Kavanagh.

[314] CSSR PA London, Domestic Chronicles of St Mary's Clapham. Biography: Fr. Kavanagh.

[315] CSSR PA London, Domestic Chronicles of St Mary's Clapham. Biography: Fr. Kavanagh.

[316] Ibid.

[317] Ibid.

[318] CSSR PA London, Domestic Chronicles of St Mary's Clapham. Biography: Fr. Kavanagh.

[319] Ibid.

[320] Ibid.

[321] CSSR PA London, Domestic Chronicles of St Mary's Clapham. Biography: Fr.

Kavanagh.

[322] Ibid.

[323] Ibid.

[324] Ibid.

[325] CSSR PA London, Domestic Chronicles of St Mary's Clapham. Biography: Fr. Kavanagh.

[326] CSSR PA London, Domestic Chronicles of St Mary's Clapham. Biography: Fr. Kavanagh.

[327] CSSR PA London, Domestic Chronicles of St Mary's Clapham. Biography: Fr. Kavanagh.

[328] CSSR PA London, Domestic Chronicles of St Mary's Clapham. Biography: Fr. Kavanagh.

[329] CSSR PA London, Domestic Chronicles of St Mary's Clapham. Biography: Fr. Kavanagh.

[330] CSSR PA London, Domestic Chronicles of St Mary's Clapham. Biography: Fr. Kavanagh.

[331] Ibid.

[332] CSSR PA London, Domestic Chronicles of St Mary's Clapham. Biography: Fr. Kavanagh.

[333] Ibid.

[334] CSSR PA London, Domestic Chronicles of St Mary's Clapham. Biography: Fr. Kavanagh.

[335] Ibid.

[336] CSSR PA London, Domestic Chronicles of St Mary's Clapham. Biography: Fr. Kavanagh.

[337] Ibid.

[338] CSSR PA London, Domestic Chronicles of St Mary's Clapham. Biography: Fr. Kavanagh.

[339] Ibid.

[340] CSSR PA London, Domestic Chronicles of St Mary's Clapham. Biography: Fr. Kavanagh.

[341] CSSR PA London, Domestic Chronicles of St Mary's Clapham. Biography: Fr. Kavanagh.

[342] Ibid.

[343] CSSR PA London, Domestic Chronicles of St Mary's Clapham. Biography: Fr. Kavanagh.

[344] CSSR PA London, Domestic Chronicles of St Mary's Clapham. Biography: Fr. Kavanagh.

[345] Ibid.

[346] CSSR PA London, Domestic Chronicles of St Mary's Clapham. Biography: Fr. Kavanagh.

[347] Ibid.

[348] CSSR PA London, Domestic Chronicles of St Mary's Clapham. Biography: Fr. Kavanagh.

[349] CSSR PA London, Domestic Chronicles of St Mary's Clapham. Biography: Fr. Kavanagh.

[350] CSSR PA London, Domestic Chronicles of St Mary's Clapham. Biography: Fr. Kavanagh.

[351] CSSR PA London, Domestic Chronicles of St Mary's Clapham. Biography: Fr. Kavanagh.

[352] CSSR PA London, Domestic Chronicles of St Mary's Clapham. Biography: Fr. Kavanagh.

[353] CSSR PA London, Domestic Chronicles of St Mary's Clapham. Letter: Fr. Bridgett.

[354] CSSR PA London, Domestic Chronicles of St Mary's Clapham. Biography: Fr. Kavanagh.

[355] CSSR PA London, Domestic Chronicles of St Mary's Clapham. Biography: Fr. Kavanagh.

[356] Ibid.

[357] CSSR PA London, Domestic Chronicles of St Mary's Clapham. Biography: Fr. Kavanagh.

[358] CSSR PA London, Domestic Chronicles of St Mary's Clapham. Biography: Fr. Kavanagh.

[359] Venerable Joseph Passerat C.Ss.R., Redemptorist Saints, <www.redemptorists.co.uk> [Accessed 21 Feb 2019].

[360] CSSR PA London, Domestic Chronicles of St Mary's Clapham. Biography: Fr. Kavanagh.

[361] CSSR PA London, Domestic Chronicles of St Mary's Clapham. Entry: 18 Nov 1914.

[362] CSSR PA London, Domestic Chronicles of Bishop Eton Liverpool. Entry: May 1915.

[363] CSSR PA London, Domestic Chronicles of St Mary's Clapham. Letter from Fr. Kavanagh.

[364] CSSR PA London, Domestic Chronicles of St Mary's Clapham. Letter from Fr. Kavanagh.

[365] CSSR PA London, Domestic Chronicles of St Mary's Clapham. Letter from R.J. Pendell.

[366] CSSR PA London, Domestic Chronicles of St Mary's Clapham. Telegram from Fr. Provincial.

[367] CSSR PA London, Domestic Chronicles of St Mary's Clapham. Letter from Private. Hitchens.

[368] CSSR PA London, Domestic Chronicles of St Mary's Clapham. Letter from Private. Hitchens.

[369] CSSR PA London, Domestic Chronicles of St Mary's Clapham. Letter from Private. Hitchens.

[370] CSSR PA London, Domestic Chronicles of St Mary's Clapham. Letter from Captain Royal Artillery.

[371] CSSR PA London, Domestic Chronicles of St Mary's Clapham. Letter from Staff-Captain Bernard J. Smith.

[372] CSSR PA London, Domestic Chronicles of St Mary's Clapham. Letter from the front.

[373] CSSR PA London, Domestic Chronicles of St Mary's Clapham. Letter from the front.

[374] CSSR PA London, Domestic Chronicles of St Mary's Clapham. Letter from Sergeant RAMC.

[375] CSSR PA London, Domestic Chronicles of St Mary's Clapham. Letter from Chaplain Donnell C.F.

[376] CSSR PA London, Domestic Chronicles of St Mary's Clapham. Letter from Chaplain Donnell C.F.

[377] Ibid.

[378] CSSR PA London, Domestic Chronicles of St Mary's Clapham. Letter from Chaplain Donnell C.F.

[379] CSSR PA London, Domestic Chronicles of St Mary's Clapham. Letter from a chaplain.

[380] CSSR PA London, Domestic Chronicles of St Mary's Clapham. Letter from a Sargent Major.

[381] CSSR PA London, Domestic Chronicles of St Mary's Clapham. Letter from a Sargent Major.

[382] CSSR PA London, Domestic Chronicles of St Mary's Clapham. Biography: Fr. Kavanagh.

[383] CSSR PA London, Domestic Chronicles of St Mary's Clapham. Biography: Fr. Conroy.

[384] CSSR PA London, Domestic Chronicles of St Mary's Clapham. Biography: Fr. Conroy.

[385] Ibid.

[386] CSSR PA London, Domestic Chronicles of St Mary's Clapham. Biography: Fr.

Conroy.

[387] CSSR PA London, Domestic Chronicles of St Mary's Clapham. Biography: Fr. Conroy.

[388] RAF Chaplaincy Branch, Overview in RAF Chaplaincy Branch, <https://www.raf.mod.uk/our-organisation/units/raf-chaplains/> [Accessed 21 Feb 2019].

[389] RAF Chaplaincy Branch Archives, Email RE. 2TAF.

[390] CSSR PA London, Domestic Chronicles of St Mary's Clapham. Biography: Fr. Gibson.

[391] CSSR PA London, Domestic Chronicles of St Mary's Clapham. Biography: Fr. Gibson.

[392] CSSR PA London, Domestic Chronicles of St Mary's Clapham. Entry RE Coronation of HM Queen Elizabeth II.

[393] CSSR PA London, Domestic Chronicles of St Mary's Clapham. Biography: Fr. Gibson.

[394] CSSR PA London, Domestic Chronicles of St Mary's Clapham. Biography: Fr. Hull.

[395] CSSR PA London, Domestic Chronicles of St Mary's Clapham. Biography: Fr. Hull.

[396] CSSR PA London, Domestic Chronicles of St Mary's Clapham. Biography: Fr. Hull.

[397] CSSR PA London, Domestic Chronicles of St Mary's Clapham. Biography: Fr. Hull.

[398] Ibid.

[399] CSSR PA London, Domestic Chronicles of St Mary's Clapham. Biography: Fr. Hull.

[400] Ibid.

[401] CSSR PA London, Domestic Chronicles of St Mary's Clapham. Letter from Fr. General.

[402] CSSR PA London, Domestic Chronicles of St Mary's Clapham. Biography: Fr. Hull.

[403] Ibid.

[404] CSSR PA London, Domestic Chronicles of St Mary's Clapham. Biography: Fr. Hull.

[405] CSSR PA London, Domestic Chronicles of St Mary's Clapham. Biography: Fr. Hull.

[406] Fr. Bev Ahearn C.Ss.R., Memoirs of Fr. Charlton, <http://www.redemptorists.co.uk/33-who-we-are.html?start=48> [Accessed 22 Feb 2019].

[407] CSSR PA London, Domestic Chronicles of St Mary's Clapham.

[408] CSSR PA London, Domestic Chronicles of St Mary's Clapham. Biography: Fr. Charlton.

[409] CSSR PA London, Domestic Chronicles of St Mary's Clapham. Biography: Fr. Hughes.

[410] CSSR PA London, Domestic Chronicles of St Mary's Clapham. Biography: Fr. Hughes.

[411] Aggies, Aggie Weston's, <http://www.aggies.org.uk/> [Accessed 22 Feb 2019].

Made in the USA
Middletown, DE
21 August 2019